Unlock your energy
for holistic wellbeing

Practical
Chakras

Lucy Lee

Illustrated by Viki Lester

Contents

Introduction

In 2017, after coming out the other side of what felt like a lifetime of anxiety and depression, I found myself embarking upon a "year of yes."

My existence prior to this moment had been so riddled with panic (to the point I would often go through lengthy periods of not leaving the house) that to finally be awake to the miracle of being alive made me feel a sudden, urgent need to throw myself wholeheartedly into saying "yes" to life to make up for lost time.

That year entailed endless adventures that altered my life trajectory, but perhaps most life changing of all was the day I said "yes" to learning Reiki.

I did not consider myself a spiritual person and had never experienced Reiki before, so I sat through my Level 1 course, intrigued yet sceptical. Guided by my teacher, I gave myself my first energy healing treatment, which entailed hovering my hands over each chakra to infuse it with life force energy. I held my hands at my crown chakra ... and felt nothing. I moved to my third eye chakra ... and still felt nothing. Until I got to my throat chakra, when all of a sudden, everything changed. The moment my hands came to my neck I felt a burning heat surging through my hands, a searing pain swirling around my throat, and a sudden wave of sadness so intense it caused me to cry somewhat uncontrollably.

That was my first experience with chakras. It was incredibly potent for me to feel the throat energy center so viscerally, and to be a part of actively soothing and releasing the blockages that had accumulated.

From that moment on I trained over the following years to become a Reiki Master and have held hundreds of sessions to assist people in working with their chakras to bring mind, body, and spirit back into balance. It is a great privilege to hold this type of space, but I believe that, above all, you are your own greatest healer. Therefore, you do not need to be or visit a Reiki practitioner in order to work with your chakras. This book has been curated with a lot of love to give you all the tools you need to tend to yourself and bring your own chakras back into balance—empowering you to step into a life of greater harmony, vitality, and self-discovery.

What are Chakras?

The human body is not only a physical entity but is also made up of an energy body. Your energy body is made up of a vital life force known as "prana" in Sanskrit, "chi" in Chinese, or "qi" in Japanese. This life force energy flows through intricate networks that distribute energy throughout the body, ensuring that every part of us receives the necessary vitality to function optimally. At certain points along these channels, the energy concentrates into energy centers known as chakras.

Chakra is a Sanskrit word meaning "spinning wheel." There are said to be seven main chakras that govern different aspects of our physical, emotional, and spiritual health.

The History of Chakras

The concept of chakras has a deep and extensive history rooted in ancient Hindu scriptures known as the Vedas. While the Vedas themselves do not explicitly mention chakras, they introduced the idea of nadis: the intricate network of energy channels within the body through which life force energy flows. Expanding upon this concept, the Upanishads, composed between 1200 and 500 BCE, identified a complex system of seventy-two thousand nadis, highlighting three principal ones: Ida, Pingala, and Sushumna. These nadis intersect at various points along the spine, forming the foundational energy centers known as chakras.

From these ancient roots, the understanding of chakras evolved within Hindu and Yogic traditions, where they were systematically mapped and associated with specific physical, emotional, and spiritual attributes. By the 6th century, Tantric teachings further elaborated on each chakra, linking them to specific mantras, deities, and elemental forces.

The introduction of the chakra system to the Western world occurred in the late 19th and early 20th centuries, and today, the chakra system is widely embraced in holistic practices such as yoga and meditation—each applying and interpreting its principles in various ways. Despite centuries of interpretation and adaptation, the fundamental significance of chakras in relation to our physical, emotional, and spiritual wellbeing remains universally acknowledged. It is crucial to honor the rich heritage of the chakras while integrating this ancient wisdom into contemporary practices, ensuring that the depth of this knowledge is preserved and appreciated in our modern context.

The Seven Main Chakras

When our chakras are well-balanced and open, energy is able to flow freely through our bodies and we are able to access a state of energetic harmony that infuses our spiritual, emotional, and physical health. However, when our chakras are blocked or imbalanced, the flow of energy is disrupted, and this imbalance can manifest itself as physical ailments and emotional turbulence. When we understand and work with the chakra system, the rewards can profoundly impact all aspects of our lives.

Each chakra corresponds not only to specific areas within the physical body, but also to distinct emotional, spiritual, and psychological states.

Each chakra can be in one of three states: balanced, underactive, or overactive.

You can find a breakdown in each chapter of the symptoms of a balanced, underactive, or overactive chakra, and I also have included a chakra body scan on page 9 to help you identify which chakra or chakras to work with using this book.

The seven main chakras are:

Root Chakra (Muladhara)

Governs security, stability, and survival instincts.

Sacral Chakra (Svadhisthana)

Influences creativity, emotions, and sensuality.

Solar Plexus Chakra (Manipura)

Linked with self-esteem, confidence, and personal power.

Heart Chakra (Anahata)

Responsible for love, compassion, and connection with others.

Throat Chakra (Vishuddha)

Impacts communication, self-expression, and speaking our truth.

Third Eye Chakra (Ajna)

Governs intuition, wisdom, and perception.

Crown Chakra (Sahasrara)

Connects to higher consciousness, spiritual enlightenment, and the divine.

Crown Chakra (Sahasrara)

Third Eye Chakra (Ajna)

Throat Chakra (Vishuddha)

Heart Chakra (Anahata)

Solar Plexus Chakra (Manipura)

Sacral Chakra (Svadhisthana)

Root Chakra (Muladhara)

Your Chakra Balancing Toolkit

Throughout the next chapters, you will learn about each chakra's unique qualities in more detail, and will be guided through some practical exercises to nurture their alignment. Whether you are completely new to the world of chakras or seeking to further your understanding, this book offers a path to greater self-awareness, holistic wellbeing, and to living a fuller life. Your healing journey is unique to you. Therefore, this book does not need to be worked through chronologically.

Organized by chapter, you will find the following for each chakra:

Rituals relating to specific scenarios that may arise due to different chakra imbalances. These rituals serve to support your daily needs.

Mudras (sacred hand positions) that harness and direct your body's energy for balance and healing.

Mantras, a one word chant (known as a "bija mantra" or "seed sound") that correlates to the element linked to each chakra. Rather than being words holding specific meanings, bija mantras are potent sounds that contain the essence of a particular energy. The bija mantras in this book are said to resonate at a frequency that aligns with the vibrational nature of a specific element—earth, water, fire, air, and ether. This resonance creates a harmonious interaction between the mantra and the element it represents—and therefore also in its corresponding chakra.

Affirmations to establish a healthy, enriching, and loving self-narrative.

Journal Prompts designed to provoke reflection of your inner landscape and cultivate a deeper self-awareness.

Crystals to enhance your energy, promote healing, and bring you back into alignment.

Essential Oils to rejuvenate your senses and support emotional and physical wellbeing.

Caution: This book includes recipes that contain essential oils, which may not be suitable for very sensitive skin. If you have any concerns about applying any of these recipes, perform a patch test first, speak to your doctor or healthcare practitioner, or avoid these recipes. Many of these recipes include specific measurements to help you dilute the oils for application, but for any that don't, you must research how to properly dilute them before applying topically.

Chakra Body Scan

This chakra scan will help you cultivate an awareness of your energy body and help you identify which chakra to work with. When instructed to place your hands over each energy centre, tune in to any information, emotions, or sensations you pick up on. If this is your first time tuning in to your chakras and energy, the sensations and feedback you receive may be subtle. This skill will strengthen over time, so be patient.

1 Find a quiet space and sit comfortably. Close your eyes and take a few deep breaths to center yourself.

2 Gently rub your hands together to generate warmth and energy between your palms, then hold your hands a few inches apart, palms facing each other but not touching.

3 Imagine or visualize a ball of energy forming between your hands. Slowly move your hands closer together and then apart, noticing any sensations you feel between your palms. You might sense warmth, tingling, or a magnetic pull. Be patient and open to whatever sensations arise.

4 Once you can feel the energy between your hands, place your hands on your root chakra at the base of your spine. Visualize a red, glowing orb of energy at this point. Hold for 2–3 minutes.

5 Move your hands to the lower abdomen, just below the navel. Envision an orange, swirling energy ball. Hold for 2–3 minutes.

6 Place your hands on the upper abdomen, near the solar plexus. Visualize a bright yellow, radiant sphere of energy. Hold for 2–3 minutes.

7 Shift your hands to the center of your chest. Picture a green, pulsating orb of light at your heart center. Hold for 2–3 minutes.

8 Move your hands to your throat area. Envision a blue, spinning vortex of energy. Hold for 2–3 minutes.

9 Place your hands on the center of your forehead, between your eyebrows. Imagine an indigo, swirling energy center. Hold for 2–3 minutes.

10 Finally, bring your hands to the top of your head. Visualize a violet or white, radiant crown of light. Hold for 2–3 minutes.

11 Open your eyes, reflect on your experience and note down anything that feels important.

Chapter 1

The Root Chakra for Stability and Grounding

The Root Chakra

The first of the seven chakras, located just between the tailbone and the pelvic floor, the root is the foundation of the entire chakra system. The root chakra governs our basic survival needs, such as safety, security, and stability. The energy within our root determines how grounded we are within ourselves and the world.

Sanskrit Name: Muladhara

Meaning: Root

Element: Earth

Location: Base of the spine

Color: Red

When Your Root Chakra is Balanced

* You feel calm and grounded

* You have clear thinking

* You have a strong sense of self

* Life's challenges feel manageable

* You feel securely anchored in your body, in your life, and to your purpose

* Your relationships feel nourishing and secure

* Your financial, domestic, and social environments feel resourced

When Your Root Chakra is Underactive

* You often feel anxious, worried, or insecure

* You lack groundedness and feel unrooted

* You feel disconnected from the world and those around you

* You isolate yourself

* You worry about money and meeting basic needs

When Your Root Chakra is Overactive

* You are never satisfied with what you have and are always lusting for more

* You snap at people easily

* Minor inconveniences are difficult for you to let go of

* Your relationships are volatile

* You have difficulty trusting others

* Your thoughts and behaviors are rigid and resistant to change

Physical Symptoms of Root Chakra Imbalance

* Chronic fatigue or low energy levels

* Issues with the legs, feet, or lower back

* Digestive problems

* Adrenal fatigue

* Weakened immune system

* Eating disorders or emotional eating

* Increased anxiety or panic attacks

Caring for your root chakra is akin to building the foundation of your dream home. Just as a sturdy base ensures a strong and stable house, a healthy root chakra gives you the footing for the rest of the chakra system to thrive. Without this strong base, the health and balance of the other chakras are compromised.

You will need

½ tsp jojoba oil

1 drop peppermint essential oil

Your favorite high tempo music

A red crystal (like red jasper)

Soothing Somatic Ritual

You've snoozed your alarm for the fifth time and there is a growing knot of dread in your stomach. Maybe you have something significant happening today, or perhaps it's just one of those days where you've woken feeling anxious for no apparent reason. This somatic ritual will help to get you out of your head and into your body, anchoring your root chakra to help you feel more centered and balanced for your day ahead.

The Ritual

1 Get up and out of bed.

2 Congratulate yourself for completing the hardest part of this ritual.

3 Plant both feet firmly on the floor. Give a few stamps with each foot to really root your connection to the ground beneath you.

4 Combine the jojoba oil and peppermint essential oil. Rub your hands together to warm the oil.

5 Bring your hands to your nose and inhale deeply, allowing the invigorating scent of peppermint to soothe your senses.

6 Now, with the music, imagine a powerful surge of electricity is flowing through your body. The way you move is not meant to look pretty or like a dance.

7 Visualize shaking all of the stress and anxiety out of your body.

8 Shake, shake, shake for at least 3 minutes. It should leave you feeling slightly out of breath.

9 Come to a moment of stillness and place both hands at the base of your spine. Take three deep breaths into this space. Allow each breath to carry away any lingering tension.

10 When you're ready, gently bring movement back into your body and transition into your day, carrying this sense of calm with you. Consider keeping a red crystal in your pocket to help soothe and ground you.

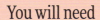

You will need

A lighter or matches

A sustainably sourced sage bundle

A red tablecloth and small table

A candle

Photos of people who feel like home to you

Crystals like smoky quartz or red jasper

Offerings from nature

Anything that feels sentimental to you

Grounding Altar Ritual

Creating an altar is an opportunity for you to carve out a place that becomes your sacred space—a place where you can come to journal, meditate, ground, pray or complete the rest of the rituals in this book. If your day has left you feeling flighty, sit for a while at your altar and come home to yourself.

The Ritual

1 Choose a location for your altar that is quiet, peaceful, and free of distractions.

2 Gather all of your materials.

3 Light your sage bundle and waft it round your altar location to cleanse the space.

4 Take a deeply nourishing breath and acknowledge that you are about to engage in a sacred ritual.

5 Drape your table with the red cloth, inviting the grounding energy of the root chakra into your space. This rich color creates a strong, supportive foundation for your altar.

6 Place your candle on your altar and light it.

7 Intuitively and mindfully place the rest of your items on your altar.

8 Come to your altar regularly as a part of your daily routine. This can be as simple as spending a few moments in reflection, lighting the candle or adding a new item that resonates with your current journey.

9 Your altar can be as minimalist or elaborate as you wish, but the priority is that it becomes a space that feels special to you.

10 Consider the following prompts when curating your altar. What energy do I want this space to radiate? What parts of myself or my life am I inviting into this sacred space for healing, growth, or reflection? How can this altar serve as a reminder of my intentions and spiritual path?

You will need

A red crystal (like red jasper)

A candle

Journal and a pen

New Beginnings
Manifestation Script

You've just landed a new job, moved into a new home, or are entering a new relationship. Whatever this next chapter of life entails, cultivating a strong and healthy root chakra is vital to ensure you can embrace the unknown with a sense of excitement rather than trepidation. This manifestation ritual welcomes change with open arms while rehearsing "expecting the best," giving your root chakra the power to set you out on each new endeavor with an optimistic mindset.

The Ritual

1 Settle in a calm and comfortable space. Clasp your red crystal with both hands and then place your hands within your lap.

2 Call to mind your new beginning and notice what emotions arise when you initially begin to think about it. Honor any fears, worries, or apprehensions you may have. Honor the part of you that may feel uncertain.

3 Begin to visualize—almost like a movie—the most perfect unfolding of this situation. Really allow yourself to indulge in your dream scenario - nothing is off limits here. What would you like to happen? How does it feel to imagine everything falling perfectly into place? Stay with this imagery until it feels complete.

4 Get your journal and pen and write down everything you visualized.

5 Tear out this page and place it somewhere you will see it often, like your work desk or your altar.

6 Take a moment to give gratitude for this moment and all the juicy possibilities your life possesses. Consider and then complete one small action you could commit to each day that aligns with the fruition of your dream new beginning.

Root Chakra Mudra

Prithvi mudra, also known as "earth mudra," is a deeply grounding gesture that enables us to connect with our physical body and cultivate a sense of groundedness and inner strength. Prithvi mudra is also said to eliminate energy deficiencies in the root chakra, which can boost alertness and increase stamina.

How to Practice Prithvi Mudra

1 Sit comfortably with your back straight and your shoulders relaxed.

2 On each hand, touch the tip of your thumb to the tip of your ring finger with a gentle yet firm pressure.

3 Keep the rest of your fingers out extended.

4 Maintaining this position, place the backs of your hands on your knees or thighs with your palms facing up.

5 Gently close your eyes or lower your gaze.

6 Begin to deepen your breath, taking slow and steady inhalations through your nose and exhaling through your

mouth. Remain in this position for a few minutes or as long as it feels comfortable.

7 Release the mudra by placing your palms down on your thighs or knees.

8 Take a moment to notice how you feel, embracing any sense of grounding and stabilizing that arises from practicing prithvi mudra.

Caution: Prithvi mudra is not recommended if you are pregnant.

Root Chakra Mantra

The mantra for the earth element, which corresponds to the root chakra, is "LAM." Chanting LAM (pronounced "lum") is said to cleanse and purify the root chakra so that life force energy can flow through it freely. If prana is flowing unobstructed through the root chakra, it allows us to establish feelings of groundeness and connection to the physical world.

How to Chant LAM

1 Sit in a comfortable position. If possible, keep your spine erect to allow your life force energy to flow freely.

2 Close your eyes and begin to draw your attention inward. Bring your awareness to the base of your spine, where the root chakra is located.

3 Visualize a red spinning wheel of energy at this point.

4 Start chanting the mantra LAM aloud. Chant it at a comfortable pitch and volume, and let the sound resonate deeply within you.

5 As you chant, feel the vibration of the sound LAM resonating at the base of your spine. Imagine this vibration clearing and energizing your root chakra, bringing it into balance.

6 Continue chanting the mantra for 5–10 minutes.

7 After chanting, take a moment to sit quietly and observe any sensations, thoughts, or emotions that arise.

Root Chakra Affirmations

Use these root chakra affirmations in moments when you feel unsettled, or use daily to begin to anchor into a more balanced way of relating to yourself. Greet all of the emotions that arise with these affirmations with a gentle curiosity. Are there any affirmations you have an uneasy reaction to? What needs to change in your life for these statements to feel true?

I am grounded.

I am safe in my body.

My body is my home.

My mind feels clear and focused.

I feel anchored in the
present moment.

I have the power to overcome
challenging moments.

My resilience allows me to adapt
with ease to change.

I trust in myself and my life.

All is well in my world.

I have everything I need.

I will always find peace in the
present moment.

Money flows to me with ease.

I am always provided for.

The universe has my back and I
have my own back.

Root Chakra Essential Oils

These woody and rich essential oils are the perfect remedy for promoting a sense of stability and enhancing your connection to your physical body. By integrating these essential oils into your daily practices, you can cultivate a solid foundation from which to build a balanced and empowered life.

Cedarwood is your anchor in the storm. Earthy and grounding, it stimulates a sense of calm and alleviates stress. This essential oil can help you to feel rooted no matter what life throws your way.

Black Pepper has a soothing and warming scent that can promote feelings of calm during times of unease. It's also said to support the functioning of the adrenal glands, which play a big part in the functioning of a healthy root chakra.

Vetiver is said to be one of the go-to essential oils in moments of shock or trauma. Heavy and earthy in scent, it soothes the mind and provides a sense of grounding when emotions may be running high.

Cypress essential oil can aid in alleviating feelings of anxiety or nervousness by deeply rooting you back into the present moment. Fresh and invigorating, it can also keep you feel energized throughout your day.

Ideas for Use

* Dilute a few drops of essential oil in a few tablespoons of carrier oil (like jojoba or coconut oil) and apply to the base of the spine during any of the root chakra rituals in this book.

* Add a few drops of essential oils to an aromatherapy diffuser. Inhale the grounding scents to promote a sense of stability throughout your day.

* Dilute essential oils with a carrier oil and give yourself a grounding foot massage before bed, or before taking a grounding barefoot walk on grass to connect with the earth and promote relaxation.

Chapter 2

The Sacral Chakra for Creativity and Passion

The Sacral Chakra

Positioned just below the navel, the sacral chakra is our second chakra and is the center of our creativity, emotions, and sensuality. It influences our ability to experience pleasure and intimacy, governing our spiritual and emotional wellbeing.

Sanskrit Name: Svadhisthana

Meaning: The Seat of the Self

Element: Water

Location: Lower abdomen

Color: Orange

When Your Sacral Chakra is Balanced

* You feel your creativity flowing freely

* You have a zest for life and embrace experiences with enthusiasm and vitality

* You honor your emotions

* You have a heightened awareness and enjoyment of physical pleasures and intimacy

* You find joy in nurturing yourself and others, fostering deep and meaningful connections

When Your Sacral Chakra is Underactive

* You find it difficult to express your emotions

* You feel emotionally numb

* You experience a creative block and lack inspiration

* You have no interest in sensual pleasures or intimacy

* You find it difficult to connect with people emotionally

* You feel guilty when thinking about your own pleasure or personal desires

When Your Sacral Chakra is Overactive

* You have intense mood swings and emotions that are difficult to manage

* You tend to overindulge in pleasures like food, sex, or substances

* You react impulsively to your emotions rather than rationally

* You have difficulty establishing boundaries in your relationships

* You may be manipulative and use charm or emotions to control others or situations

Physical Symptoms of Sacral Chakra Imbalance

* Issues with the reproductive organs

* Lower back pain or stiffness

* Digestive issues

* Low energy levels

* Urinary system issues, including frequent urinary tract infections (UTIs) or kidney problems

Nurturing the sacral chakra is akin to beginning the process of decorating your dream home. What brings you joy? What brings you pleasure? What lights you up? Are you allowing yourself to be surrounded by these things every day to nurture your own unique creative expression?

You will need

A piece of paper

Pencils

A paintbrush and paints (optional)

Felt tip markers (optional)

Creative Block Release Ritual

Within this creative session you have one core instruction: Create something rubbish. Yes, you read that correctly. Pen the worst piece of writing imaginable. Draw something terribly. Give yourself unbridled permission to create without the pressure of it having to be "good" and watch how you get out of your way, begin to open up to a more carefree expression of yourself, and delight in the sacral chakra's joyful creative potential.

The Ritual

1 Choose a space where you feel comfortable and at ease.

2 Arrange your creative materials.

3 Close your eyes and take a few deep breaths.

4 Place your hands on your lower abdomen, just below your navel, and connect to the energy center of your sacral chakra.

5 Connect to the intention of allowing yourself to create something "rubbish." Let the silliness of that intention alone bring a smile to your face.

6 Open your eyes.

7 Take a piece of paper and your creative tools of choice and begin to draw, doodle, or write—whatever takes your fancy.

8 If you feel your mind trying to over-intellectualize the process, begin to scribble and scrawl or even write the same sentence over and over. If you feel the need to start over, stick with it. This work of art is meant to be your worst yet.

9 Once you feel complete with your piece, take a moment to reflect on the experience. How did it feel to create without the pressure of it being good? Could you create without judgment? Did it feel liberating to embrace imperfection and create for creation's sake? Do you actually like how your "rubbish" art looks?

10 Place your hands back on your lower abdomen and silently, or aloud, say the affirmation: "I embrace my creativity. I create freely and joyfully."

11 Take a few deep breaths, gradually bringing your awareness back to your body and the present moment.

You will need

Fresh flower petals

Leaves

Twigs

Stones

Any natural treasures you stumble across

Healing Flower Mandala

Spending time in nature and immersing yourself within the
elements is a gateway to a state of flow and inner harmony.
The process of creating art energizes our creativity and vitality.
Combining the two together is a dream made in sacral chakra
heaven. Mindfully gathering petals and natural materials to create
a mandala helps balance and energize the sacral chakra. This
beautiful ritual can help spark your imagination whilst inviting
more joy and pleasure into your life.

The Ritual

1 Set out to go on a mindful walk
   in nature.

2 Become alive to your senses as you
   walk there. What can you hear?
   See? Smell?

3 As you walk, look out for treasures
   to collect for your flower mandala.
   Ensure you are picking elements
   that have naturally fallen to the earth
   and give a silent thanks as you
   collect them.

4 Find a quiet place on your walk to
   settle and create your art. The ground
   will become your canvas.

5 Start from the center and work
   outward. Place your petals and
   natural elements intuitively in a way
   that feels harmonious to you—there is
   no right or wrong way to do this. Allow
   your creativity to flow.

6 Once you feel complete with your
   process, sit quietly in front of your
   mandala and, taking a few deep
   breaths, bask in its beauty.

7 Close your eyes and visualize the
   vibrant orange energy of the sacral
   chakra flowing through you, out
   into your mandala, and back to you
   once more.

8 When you feel ready, slowly open
   your eyes and tune in to how it feels
   to have co-created with nature to
   produce this work of art.

9 Thank the natural elements once
   more for their contribution to your
   healing process. You can either
   disassemble your mandala or leave it
   in place for other passersby to enjoy.

You will need

Candles

A lighter or matches

An orange, water-safe crystal
(like carnelian)

1 cup (240 g) Epsom salts

Essential oil (like orange, patchouli,
jasmine, or ylang ylang)

Body oil

Emotional Release Ritual

**Disharmony in the sacral chakra can occur if you are
not fully processing your emotions. This soothing water
ritual invites you to tend to yourself, to honour your inner
landscape and release all that is no longer serving you.**

The Ritual

1 Run yourself a warm bath.

2 Dim the lights and create a calming atmosphere with candles or soft lighting.

3 Add your crystal, a cup of Epsom bath salts, and 5–10 drops of essential oils to the bathwater.

4 As you get into the bath, tune in to an intention. This could be an intention to release pent-up emotions, invite healing into your sacral chakra, or simply to nurture yourself.

5 Visualize the warm water, salts, oils, and crystal working harmoniously to cleanse and balance your sacral chakra.

6 Visualize the warm water surrounding you like a cocoon, gently washing away any emotional blockages or tension stored in your sacral chakra. Feel the healing energy of the water element restoring harmony.

7 Tune in to your emotions and where you feel them in your body. Create little waves in the water to lap over the body part that is feeling the depth of emotion or tension that may be arising. Imagine the water cleansing and washing it away.

8 When you're ready, get out of the bath and dry yourself off.

9 Take your body oil, warm it between your palms, and begin massaging your body, starting from your feet and moving upward. Focus on areas associated with the sacral chakra, such as the lower abdomen, lower back, and hips. Use gentle, circular motions to promote circulation and relaxation.

10 Do this as mindfully as you can.

Sacral Chakra Mudra

Jala mudra, also known as the "water gesture," is a mudra that symbolizes the fluidity of water. As water is the element of the sacral chakra, practicing jala mudra regularly can help cultivate a sense of fluidity in life and help attain emotional balance.

How to Practice Jala Mudra

1 Sit comfortably with your back straight and your shoulders relaxed.

2 On each hand, touch the tip of your thumb to the tip of your little finger. Keep the rest of your fingers extended and relaxed.

3 Place the backs of your hands on your knees or thighs with your palms facing upward. Allow your hands to relax in this position.

4 Gently close your eyes or lower your gaze and bring your attention inward.

5 Connect to your breath, taking slow, deep inhales and exhales.

6 Stay in this position for a few minutes, or as long as it feels good to you. Fully immerse yourself in the experience of jala mudra.

7 Release your hands and place them on your knees, palms facing down to ground your energy.

8 Slowly open your eyes and bring your awareness back to the present moment. Take a moment to notice how you feel, embracing any sense of calm or emotional balance.

Sacral Chakra Mantra

The mantra for the water element, which corresponds to the sacral chakra, is "VAM." Chanting VAM (pronounced "vum") is believed to cleanse and purify the sacral chakra, facilitating the free flow of life force energy through this energy center. When prana flows unobstructed through the sacral chakra, it enhances our ability to experience creativity, passion, and emotional balance.

How to Chant VAM

1 Sit in a comfortable position. If possible, keep your spine erect to allow your life force energy to flow freely.

2 Close your eyes and begin to draw your attention inward.

3 Bring your awareness to your lower abdomen, just below your belly button, where your sacral chakra is located.

4 Visualize a vibrant orange spinning wheel of energy at this point.

5 Begin chanting the mantra VAM aloud. Chant it at a pitch and volume that feels natural and comfortable to

you. Let the sound resonate deeply within your being.

6 As you chant VAM, imagine the sound vibrating at the sacral chakra. Visualize this vibration clearing away any blockages and revitalizing the energy center.

7 Chant the mantra continuously for 5–10 minutes.

8 After chanting, take a moment to sit quietly. Observe any sensations, thoughts, or emotions that arise within you. Reflect on how you feel energetically and emotionally.

Sacral Chakra Affirmations

For the sacral chakra, these affirmations can be employed to enhance your creativity, joy, and emotional expression. Pay attention to your feelings as you recite them. Do any affirmations resonate deeply or feel particularly empowering? How can you incorporate more moments of joy and creativity into your daily life?

I embrace my creativity and passions wholeheartedly.

I honor my emotions and allow myself to feel deeply.

I am in touch with my feelings and express them with ease.

My sensuality is a beautiful part of who I am.

I honor my sexuality.

I nurture myself and others with kindness and love.

I am worthy of experiencing life's pleasures.

I am comfortable in my own skin.

I create healthy boundaries and respect the boundaries of others.

I allow myself to enjoy life fully.

I am a creative being, and my ideas are worthy of exploration.

My relationships are supportive, loving, and respectful.

I honor the sacredness of my body.

I embrace change and allow it to transform me for the better.

My life is full of passion and zest.

Sacral Chakra Journal Prompts

These journaling prompts invite you to explore and deepen your connection to your creativity, emotions, and relationships. By engaging with these prompts, you can uncover any areas where you may feel blocked or disconnected from your creative and emotional flow, and begin to cultivate a greater sense of joy, passion, and intimacy in your life.

* How do you feel emotionally at this moment?

* What emotions are you not allowing yourself to feel fully?

* What is one thing you could do today to honor yourself and your feelings?

* What activities make you feel inspired and ignite your creativity?

* What were your favorite hobbies as a child?

* What things could you do now as an adult that help you tap into that childlike, playful energy?

* Reflect upon a time that you felt your creativity was truly ignited. What were the conditions that contributed to you feeling this way?

* Go back to a time that you felt creatively blocked. What helped you unblock?

* What brings you pleasure?

* Which areas of your life need more passion?

* Which relationships in your life bring you joy? Note the reasons they do so.

* Which relationships in your life drain your energy?

* What boundaries need to be put in place to manage them?

* Do you feel connected to your sexual energy?

* How could you connect more intimately with your own sensual and sexual energy?

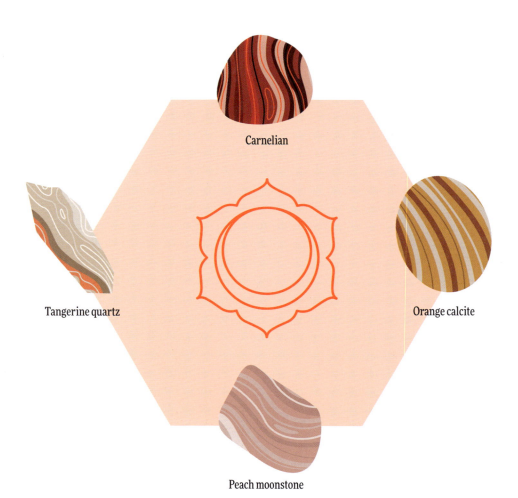

Carnelian

Tangerine quartz

Orange calcite

Peach moonstone

Sacral Chakra Crystals

The warm, orange tones of sacral chakra crystals exude energies that amplify creativity, passion, and a sense of equanimity. These crystals support the flow of creative and sensual energies within the body, helping to dispel emotional blockages, ignite inspiration, and aid you in expressing your authentic self.

Carnelian is renowned for its capacity to increase energy, vitality, and motivation. This vibrant crystal inspires creativity, strengthens courage, and encourages positive decision-making.

Orange Calcite is prized for its healing properties that invigorate and uplift the spirit. This crystal stimulates creativity, enhances optimism, and supports emotional healing, fostering a sense of joy and vitality in its users.

Peach Moonstone is valued for its gentle yet powerful healing properties. This crystal promotes inner peace, enhances intuition, and supports nurturing qualities, making it ideal for fostering compassion and self-discovery.

Tangerine Quartz possesses vibrant healing properties that stimulate creativity and passion. This crystal energizes the sacral chakra, promoting a sense of vitality and enthusiasm while encouraging exploration of one's creative potential.

Ideas for Use

* Hold the sacral chakra crystal in your hand and envision its energy infusing your lower abdomen, where the sacral chakra is centered.

* Use a smooth sacral chakra crystal to gently massage your lower abdomen in circular motions to stimulate energy flow and release blockages.

* Place the crystal on your desk while working on creative projects or near your workspace to stimulate creativity and passion. Affirm its supportive energy to enhance your creative flow and emotional balance throughout the day.

Orange essential oil

Jasmine essential oil

Ylang ylang essential oil

Patchouli essential oil

Sacral Chakra Essential Oils

When it comes to nurturing the sacral chakra,
certain fruity and floral oils can help foster creativity,
emotional balance, and a deeper sense of pleasure. By
incorporating these essential oils into your daily routine,
you can nurture a balanced sacral chakra, paving the way
for a more fulfilling and creatively abundant life.

Orange essential oil is like a burst of sunshine for your soul. Vibrant and joyful, it lifts mood, enhances joy, and fuels your passion for life, making every moment feel bright and exciting.

Ylang Ylang essential oil is sweet and floral with a musky undertone. Simultaneously soothing and stimulating, it works to reawaken passion and creativity.

Patchouli essential oil is earthy and grounding, and is known for being an aphrodisiac that can aid you in connecting to your deepest desires. It can help balance emotions and encourages sensuality, helping you embrace your authentic self with confidence.

Jasmine is sweet and sensual, and this floral essential oil can awaken your inner goddess. It boosts confidence, stirs creativity, and enhances sensuality, making you feel radiant and irresistible.

Ideas for Use

* Add a few drops of essential oil to your favorite unscented body lotion or cream. Apply it to your skin, paying special attention to your lower abdomen, to promote a sense of harmony and connection to your sensual self.

* Place a few drops of essential oil into the steam of your morning shower. As the steam rises, breathe in the scent to invigorate your senses and to set an energetic, balanced tone for the day.

* Apply a few drops of essential oil to a diffuser bracelet or necklace. Wearing scented jewelry allows you to carry the balancing energy of the essential oil with you throughout the day.

Chapter 3

The Solar Plexus Chakra for Confidence and Power

The Solar Plexus Chakra

Located in the upper abdomen, the solar plexus chakra is the seat of personal power, self-confidence, and willpower. It governs our sense of identity, autonomy, and ability to take action in the world.

Sanskrit Name: Manipura

Meaning: City of Jewels

Element: Fire

Location: Upper abdomen, above the navel

Color: Yellow

When Your Solar Plexus Chakra is Balanced

* You feel confident in yourself

* You have a strong sense of self-assurance and empowerment when facing difficulties

* You have vitality and motivation to pursue your goals with enthusiasm and determination

* You have clarity in setting goals and making decisions

* You have the ability to bounce back from setbacks

When Your Solar Plexus Chakra is Underactive

* You lack self-confidence and feel powerless when facing challenges

* You struggle with making decisions and taking action due to fear of failure

* You experience low energy and lack motivation to pursue your goals

* You avoid conflict and challenges

When Your Solar Plexus Chakra is Overactive

* You feel the need to dominate situations and others to maintain a sense of power

* You are quick to anger and react defensively to perceived threats or challenges

* You constantly strive to outperform others to prove your worth

* You set excessively high standards for yourself and others, leading to perfectionism

* You often neglect your own personal wellbeing

Physical Symptoms of Solar Plexus Chakra Imbalance

* Digestive issues like indigestion, acid reflux, or stomach ulcers

* Eating disorders or imbalances in appetite

* Chronic fatigue or adrenal fatigue

* Issues with the liver, pancreas, or gallbladder

* Muscle tension in the abdomen or lower back

Caring for the solar plexus chakra is like keeping your dream home well-lit and well-heated. Just as a well-lit and well-heated home provides warmth, comfort, and illumination, a balanced solar plexus chakra fuels your inner fire, allows you to feel comfortable within yourself, and illuminates your path, allowing you to confidently stride in the direction of your dreams.

You will need

A glass jar

Decorations for your jar
(like glass paint, jewels, stickers, or ribbons)

Sticky notes and a pen

Self-Celebration Jar

In this ritual, you will create a self-celebration jar. This is
a simple yet powerful practice to help you pause, reflect,
and appreciate all the things that make you brilliant.
By regularly engaging in the process of honoring your
accomplishments, you help to reinforce a positive
self-image, which empowers your personal will and
enhances the radiant energy of your solar plexus.

The Ritual

1   Gather your jar and all of
    your decorations.

2   Take the time to adorn your jar with
    your decorations. The act of playfully
    personalizing your jar will infuse it
    with a joyful energy and make it a
    cherished object for your celebration
    practice. Once your jar is complete,
    you are ready to begin filling it.

3   Each evening before bed, take a
    moment to reflect on your day.
    Bring to mind three things you want
    to celebrate yourself for from your
    day. Did you face and overcome a
    challenge? Did you take a step toward
    a goal? Or perhaps you brightened
    someone's day with a kind gesture?
    There is nothing too big or too small
    to celebrate yourself for.

4   Take three sticky notes and, on each
    one, write one thing you are proud
    of yourself for, or something you
    achieved today.

5   Fold the notes up and place them
    inside your jar.

6   Keep your celebration jar in a place
    where you will see it daily. Watching it
    fill up is a tangible visual reminder of
    just how amazing you are.

7   Once your jar is full, read through
    each note. Let yourself feel the
    weight of every beautiful memory,
    accomplishment, and experience.
    Reflect on the incredible journey
    you've been on and honor all the
    wonderful moments that have
    shaped you into who you are today.

You will need

Comfortable clothing

A mirror

Energizing music

Journal and pen

Radiate Confidence Ritual

Feeling unsure of yourself? Struggling with self-doubt or
low confidence? This invigorating routine is designed to
awaken your inner strength and boost your self-esteem.
Use this sequence whenever you need a confidence
boost or daily to keep your energy and self-belief sky
high. Get ready to ignite your inner fire and radiate
confidence in every aspect of your life!

The Ritual

1 Wearing comfortable clothing, stand in front of your mirror and begin to take several deep, grounding breaths.

2 Look into the mirror and make eye contact with yourself. Say aloud: "I am confident. I am powerful. I am worthy."

3 Put on your favorite energizing music and begin to move your body freely. Let go of any self-consciousness and focus on the joy of movement.

4 As you dance, begin to call to mind a moment in time where you felt most confident. Where were you? How did it feel to embody this feeling? What elements in that moment empowered you?

5 Envision how carrying this confidence might influence your decisions for the rest of the day. What would your day look like? How would you carry yourself? How might it shape the way you interact with others?

6 When you feel ready, pause your dance and return to your reflection. Once again, make direct eye contact and declare boldly: "I embody confidence. I radiate power. I am inherently worthy." Let the energy of these affirmations settle deeply within your being.

7 Feel free to continue dancing, or, turn to your journal to write down any insights, commitments or actions that will help you to maintain and radiate confidence in all that you do.

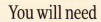

You will need

16 fl oz (470 ml) water in a saucepan

1 tsp grated fresh ginger

1 tsp turmeric powder

Pinch of ground black pepper

A lemon

Honey or sweetener to taste

Your favorite mug

Invigorating Tonic Recipe

An underactive solar plexus chakra can often be the root cause of digestive issues and low energy levels. If your digestion feels sluggish or your mood is down, this tincture can help ignite your inner fire. Drinking this tincture first thing in the morning is a guaranteed way to kickstart your digestion and boost your vitality for the day ahead.

The Ritual

1 Heat the water in a saucepan on the stove.

2 Sprinkle in your ginger, turmeric, and black pepper and stir it mindfully into the water with a lot of love.

3 Bring the mixture to a boil and then reduce the heat to allow it to simmer gently for 10–15 minutes.

4 Let the mixture cool slightly.

5 Add your lemon juice and honey.

6 Pour into your mug and enjoy your tea, knowing this fiery sunshiney concoction is stimulating your solar plexus.

Solar Plexus Chakra Mudra

Rudra mudra, also known as the "gesture to strength," is the mudra directly correlated with the solar plexus chakra, as it is said to generate great amounts of energy to stimulate greater self-confidence and willpower.

How to Practice Rudra Mudra

1 Sit comfortably, ensuring your spine is straight and your shoulders are relaxed.

2 On each hand, touch the tip of your thumb, index finger, and ring finger together. Keep your middle finger and little finger straight and extended.

3 Place your hands on your knees or thighs, with your palms facing upward. Allow your hands to relax in this position.

4 Gently close your eyes or lower your gaze and bring your attention inward.

5 Connect to your breath, taking slow, deep inhales and exhales.

6 Stay in this position for a few minutes or as long as it feels comfortable.

7 Gently release the mudra by placing your hands palms down on your thighs or knees.

8 Take a moment to notice how you feel, embracing any sense of confidence, inner strength, or vitality that arises from practicing rudra mudra.

Solar Plexus Chakra Mantra

The mantra for the fire element, which corresponds to the solar plexus chakra, is "RAM." Chanting RAM (pronounced "rum") is believed to cleanse and purify the solar plexus chakra, facilitating the free flow of life force energy through this energy center. When prana flows unobstructed through the solar plexus chakra, it enhances our sense of personal power, confidence, and inner strength.

How to Chant RAM

1   Sit in a comfortable position. If possible, keep your spine erect to allow your life force energy to flow freely.

2   Close your eyes and begin to draw your attention inward. Bring your awareness to your upper abdomen, just above your belly button where the solar plexus chakra is located.

3   Visualize a yellow spinning wheel of energy at this point.

4   Start chanting the mantra RAM aloud. Chant it at a comfortable pitch and volume. Let the sound resonate deeply within you.

5   As you chant, feel the vibration of the sound RAM resonating just above your navel. Imagine this vibration clearing and energizing your solar plexus chakra, bringing it into balance.

6   Continue chanting the mantra for at least 5–10 minutes.

7   After chanting, take a moment to sit quietly and observe any sensations, thoughts, or emotions that arise.

Solar Plexus Chakra Affirmations

When focusing on the solar plexus chakra, use these affirmations to boost your confidence, personal power, and motivation. Reflect on how these statements make you feel. Do they inspire a sense of determination and inner strength? What actions can you take to align your life more closely with these affirmations?

I feel calm, confident, and capable.

I trust in myself and my decisions.

My personal power is limitless.

I place my happiness in my own hands.

I am worthy of achieving my greatest dreams.

I genuinely celebrate others' wins and successes.

I release the need for approval from others and trust my own guidance.

I let go of limiting beliefs that hold me back.

I am a powerful creator.

I am proud of myself.

My inner resilience carries me through all of life's challenges.

I have the power to create the life I desire.

I embrace new opportunities.

I am equipped with everything I need to succeed.

Solar Plexus Chakra Journal Prompts

These journaling prompts are an invitation for you to explore and strengthen your sense of personal power, confidence, and self-discipline. By engaging with these prompts, you can boost your self-esteem, uncover any areas where you may feel powerless or lack motivation, and begin to consolidate a stronger, more empowered sense of self.

* What does personal power mean to you?

* Do you feel connected to your own power?

* Write about a time you felt truly confident in your own skin. What contributed to this feeling?

* What would you do if you weren't afraid to fail?

* What habits could you cultivate to boost your resilience and ability to bounce back from challenging situations?

* Where in your life do you feel unempowered? What actions could you take to bolster your sense of power in these areas?

* What are you most proud of yourself for? Name your biggest strengths and talents.

* What goals would you like to achieve in the next five years?

* What small steps can you take this week to make these goals a reality?

* How do you respond to being critiqued by others? How does this impact your self-esteem?

* Who is the most confident person you know? What traits do they have that you would like to cultivate?

* Reflect on a time you stepped outside of your comfort zone. What did you learn about yourself through that experience?

* What limiting beliefs or self-doubts do you need to release in order to fully embrace your personal power?

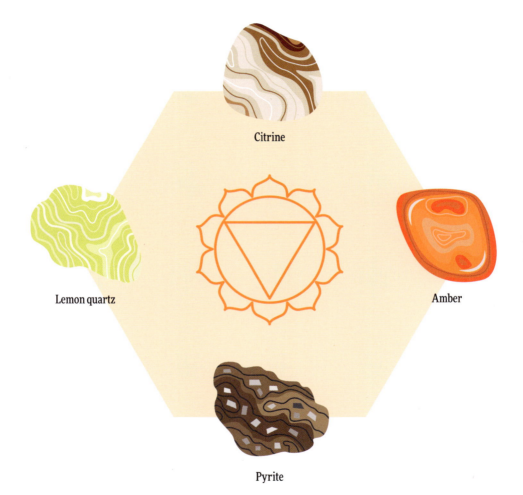

Citrine

Lemon quartz

Amber

Pyrite

Solar Plexus Chakra Crystals

Characterized by vibrant yellow hues, the crystals aligned with the solar plexus energy center amplify your personal power and inner confidence. Utilizing these crystals can help eradicate self-doubt and empower you to manifest your ambitions with clarity and purpose.

Citrine is renowned for its uplifting and energizing healing properties, promoting positivity and abundance. This radiant crystal is believed to attract prosperity, enhance creativity, and infuse the spirit with optimism and joy.

Amber is cherished for its healing properties that resonate deeply with the solar plexus chakra. This fossilized resin is believed to enhance confidence, promote vitality, and restore balance to the seat of personal power and self-esteem.

Pyrite, known as "fool's gold," is prized for its healing properties that promote vitality and manifestation. This golden mineral enhances willpower, fosters confidence, and stimulates creativity, making it an ideal companion for achieving ambitious goals.

Lemon Quartz is celebrated for its healing properties that invigorate the mind and spirit. This vibrant crystal is believed to enhance clarity, uplift mood, and promote positivity, making it a valuable tool for boosting confidence and attracting abundance.

Ideas for Use

* Hold the solar plexus chakra crystal in your hand and visualize its energy radiating into your abdomen, where the solar plexus chakra resides.

* Place one of these crystals inside your self-celebration jar (see page 51). Each time you add or read from the jar, hold on to your crystal to further amplify your commitment and dedication to building your self-belief.

* Wear the crystal as jewelry or keep it in your pocket to enhance your confidence and inner strength throughout the day, affirming its supportive energy to boost your assertiveness and clarity of purpose.

Lemon essential oil

Cinnamon essential oil

Bergamot essential oil

Ginger essential oil

Solar Plexus Chakra Essential Oils

Essential oils for the solar plexus chakra can help to ignite your inner fire, providing the motivation and clarity needed to show up to life with vivacity. When used mindfully, these oils can support the harmonization of this chakra, helping you to embrace your personal strength and shine your light defiantly.

Lemon essential oil sparks your inner sunshine. Zesty and uplifting, it energizes your spirit, boosts confidence, and sharpens focus, making you feel bright and unstoppable.

Bergamot essential oil is cheerful and refreshing, and works to banish stress, leaving you feeling balanced, confident, and ready to take on the world.

Ginger essential oil ignites your inner fire. Bold and invigorating, it fuels motivation, enhances courage, and promotes a can-do attitude, empowering you to chase your dreams fearlessly.

Cinnamon essential oil fuels your inner power. Warm and spicy, it boosts vitality, strengthens resolve, and sparks creativity, helping you embrace your personal power with passion and enthusiasm.

Ideas for Use

* Create a ritual where you apply diluted essential oils to your solar plexus area while repeating the affirmations on page 58. This combines the aromatic benefits of the oils with the power of positive intention.

* Add a few drops of diluted essential oils to your yoga practice space. During poses that engage the core or focus on personal strength (like warrior poses), the aroma can enhance your connection to the solar plexus chakra.

* Find a candle that contains one of the relevant solar plexus chakra essential oils and light it at your desk whenever you need a fragrant empowering boost while you are working.

Chapter 4

The Heart Chakra for Love and Compassion

The Heart Chakra

Positioned at the center of the chest, the heart chakra is the bridge between the lower chakras (related to earthly matters) and the upper chakras (related to spiritual aspirations). It governs our ability to love unconditionally, show compassion, and form meaningful relationships.

Sanskrit Name: Anahata

Meaning: Unhurt, unstruck, unbeaten

Element: Air

Location: Center of the chest

Color: Green or pink

When Your Heart Chakra is Balanced

* You feel a deep sense of love and empathy toward yourself and others

* You can let go of past hurts and grievances, fostering inner peace

* You experience balanced emotions, creating harmonious relationships

When Your Heart Chakra is Underactive

* You find it difficult to form meaningful connections and may feel lonely

* You are emotionally distant and struggle to express or receive love openly

* You lack empathy toward others' feelings and struggles

* You hold on to grudges and find it hard to forgive yourself and others

* You have a fear of rejection

When Your Heart Chakra is Overactive

* You put other people's needs before your own to an unhealthy extent

* You seek validation and approval from others excessively

* You feel possessive or envious of others' relationships or successes

* You overwhelm others with affection or care

* You neglect your own needs in favor of fulfilling others' desires

Physical Symptoms of Heart Chakra Imbalance

* Heart palpitations or irregular heartbeat

* Respiratory issues like asthma or allergies

* High blood pressure or hypertension

* Issues with the circulatory system or cardiac conditions

Caring for the heart chakra is like nurturing the garden in our dream home. Just as a well-tended garden blossoms with beautiful, vibrant plants and flowers, a balanced heart chakra blossoms with love, compassion, and emotional equilibrium.

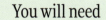

You will need

1.4 oz (40 g) shea butter

1.6 oz (45 g) solid coconut oil

1 oz (30 g) jojoba wax

A heatproof bowl

3 drops rose essential oil

3 drops lavender essential oil

Dried rose petals (optional, for decoration)

Small jar or container

Heart Connection Balm

How is your heart today? What does it need? The process of making and using this heart connection balm is a beautiful way to reconnect with yourself and your heart chakra. Scent is one of the fastest ways to change emotional state and this balm is infused with essential oils known for their heart opening properties. Lovingly massaging this balm into your chest area is a precious ritual to self-soothe, invite in feelings of love, and cultivate a deeper sense of understanding with yourself.

The Recipe

1 Place the shea butter, coconut oil, and jojoba wax into a heatproof bowl.

2 Place the bowl over a pan of boiling water and heat gently until the oils and wax have melted.

3 Remove the bowl from the heat.

4 Stir the essential oils and dried rose petals into the oil while repeating the affirmations from page 76 to infuse the balm with your loving intentions.

5 Pour the mixture into a glass jar and leave to cool and set.

The Ritual

1 Choose a quiet, comfortable space and take a few deep breaths. Breathe in through the nose, and exhale through the mouth.

2 Begin to rub your Heart Connection Balm onto your chest with the most love and presence you can. You are precious. Tend to yourself in a way that reflects this.

3 Inhale the aroma deeply.

4 Close your eyes and continue to gently massage your chest.

5 Ask yourself: "How is my heart today?" Allow thoughts or feelings to surface without judgment.

6 Now, ask: "What is it that I need?" Be open to the response. Whether it's rest, to enforce boundaries or to offer forgiveness—simply listen to the callings of your heart.

7 When you feel complete, open your eyes and reflect on what came up for you. Can you make a commitment to fulfil whatever your heart has asked of you?

You will need

All the love you can possibly muster

Paper and a pen

Beaming Love to the World Prayer

Watching the news for more than five minutes and witnessing the atrocities occurring worldwide can feel almost too much to bear. Through this prayer and ritual, you will begin to channel the limitless love within you to energize your heart center and empower you to feel capable of taking action to make a positive change in the world.

The Ritual

1 Close your eyes and take the deepest breath you've taken all day.

2 Place your hands over your heart and imagine a warm, green light emanating from the center of your chest. With each breath, imagine the green light growing stronger. Allow this light to fill your entire body, bringing a sense of peace and warmth.

3 Silently, say to yourself: "May I be filled with love. May I be happy. May I be at peace." Repeat several times and allow yourself to feel the love.

4 Visualize someone you care about and direct the green light from your heart toward theirs.

5 Silently, say: "May you be filled with love. May you be happy. May you be at peace." Repeat several times, feeling the love and compassion flowing toward them.

6 Take your time to slowly expand your visualization to include your community, your country, and finally, the entire world. See the green light from your heart flowing outward, encompassing all beings.

7 Silently, say: "May all beings be filled with love. May all beings be happy. May all beings be at peace." Repeat several times, imagining this love enveloping the entire world.

8 Take a deep breath and place your hands in a prayer position in front of your heart. Spend a few moments thinking about and writing down how you can contribute to your community in the coming weeks.

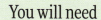

You will need

8 fl oz (235 ml) water or plant-based milk

1–2 tbsp ethically sourced, ceremonial cacao

Natural sweetener (like honey or agave)

Your favorite mug

Pen and two pieces of paper

An envelope

A postage stamp

Heartfelt Cacao and Love Letter Ritual

Have you ever dreamed of receiving a love letter? Why wait a second longer—fulfill this dream for yourself. By integrating the heart-opening properties of cacao with the intimate act of writing, you create a sacred space for self-reflection and emotional healing. Repeat this ritual whenever you need a reminder of your worth, love, and the beauty of heartfelt connections.

The Ritual

1 In a small saucepan, heat the water or plant-based milk over low heat. As the liquid warms, add 1–2 tablespoons of raw cacao powder.

2 Hold love in your heart and imagine it being infused into your drink as you stir the cacao until it has fully dissolved. Add a natural sweetener to taste. Adjust the sweetness to suit your preference.

3 Pour your cacao drink into your favorite mug.

4 Close your eyes and inhale the cacao's rich aroma. With each sip, feel it nourishing your body and opening your heart. Savor it.

5 After enjoying your cacao, sit comfortably with your pen and paper.

6 Call to mind someone special to you. Begin to write them a letter to let them know how special they are to you.

7 Once finished, take your second piece of paper and address it to yourself. Begin to write all the things you love about yourself. Get specific. Write yourself something straight out of a romance novel. Swamp yourself in your love.

8 Place your own letter on your altar or a safe place and return to it whenever you need a little boost.

9 Send your loved one their letter and smile, knowing that you have just made their world a little brighter.

Heart Chakra Mudra

Anjali mudra, also known as "prayer pose," is a
hand gesture symbolic of respect, gratitude, and
reverence. Practicing anjali mudra regularly can
help cultivate a sense of inner peace, love, and
connection, making it a powerful gesture for tuning
in to your heart space to center yourself.

How to Practice Anjali Mudra

1 Sit comfortably and ensure
your spine is straight with your
shoulders relaxed.

2 Bring your palms together in front of
your chest in a prayer-like position.

3 Press your palms firmly but gently
together, with your fingers
pointing upward.

4 Allow the base of your thumbs to
touch the center of your chest.

5 Close your eyes or lower your gaze.

6 Feel the connection of your thumbs
in your heart center and begin to
connect to your breath.

7 Stay in this position for a few minutes
or as long as it feels good to you.

8 Gently release your hands and place
them on your knees.

9 Slowly open your eyes and bring
your awareness back to the
present moment.

10 Bask in any feelings of connection
and love that arose from practicing
anjali mudra.

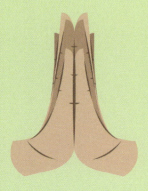

Heart Chakra Mantra

The mantra for the air element, which corresponds to the heart chakra, is "YAM." Chanting YAM (pronounced "yum") is believed to cleanse and purify the heart chakra, facilitating the free flow of life force energy through this energy center. When prana flows unobstructed through the heart chakra, it enhances our ability to give and receive love, compassion, and empathy.

How to Chant YAM

1   Sit in a comfortable position. If possible, keep your spine erect to allow your life force energy to flow freely.

2   Close your eyes and begin to draw your attention inward. Bring your awareness to the center of your chest, where the heart chakra is located.

3   Visualize a green spinning wheel of energy at this point.

4   Start chanting the mantra YAM aloud. Chant it at a comfortable pitch and volume. Let the sound resonate deeply within you.

5   As you chant, feel the vibration of the sound YAM resonating in the center of your chest. Imagine this vibration clearing and energizing your heart chakra, bringing it into balance.

6   Continue chanting the mantra for 5–10 minutes.

7   After chanting, take a moment to sit quietly and observe any sensations, thoughts, or emotions that arise.

Heart Chakra Affirmations

These heart chakra affirmations are a powerful tool to cultivate love, compassion, and emotional healing. Notice how your heart feels as you speak these words aloud or silently. What sensations arise in your heart space? Do you believe the words as you speak them? Can you fully allow yourself to receive the love that these affirmations hold?

I am worthy of all the love this world has to offer.

My heart is open to give love unconditionally.

My heart is open to receive love unconditionally.

I treasure and accept myself for all that I am.

I am thankful for all the blessings that surround me.

I forgive and release all moments I have been hurt.

I let go of all that no longer serves me.

I know and trust that love will always find me.

Loving myself is my birthright.

My heart is healed and whole.

I trust in the callings of my heart.

I am interconnected with all beings.

I honor all that my heart has been through.

I cultivate loving energy that is felt wherever I go.

I believe that embodying love can make a difference in the world.

Heart Chakra Journal Prompts

These journaling prompts are designed to help you tune in to the inner workings of your heart space to attain a deeper understanding of how this chakra is governing your life. By engaging with these prompts, you can illuminate the ways in which you desire to be loved and how you can tap into your heart's fullest potential.

* How is your heart today?

* What is it that it needs?

* What are ten things that you love about yourself?

* How do you express love toward yourself and others?

* In what ways do you want to be loved?

* How do you nurture and care for yourself emotionally, physically, mentally, and spiritually?

* Describe a relationship in your life that makes you feel loved. What qualities make this relationship so special?

* Reflect on any past hurts that have affected your ability to keep your heart open. How can you work toward healing these wounds? What did you learn from this experience?

* What would it mean for you to live with an open heart?

* What are you grateful for right now?

* Describe your ideal vision for a world filled with love, compassion, and understanding. What tangible steps can you take in your own life to make this vision a reality?

* Plan an entire day where everything you do, and every decision you make is made in complete devotion to yourself. How would you spend your time? Where would you go? What would you do?

* Write a letter to your heart. What would you say to it?

* Imagine your heart can speak. What do you think it would say to you?

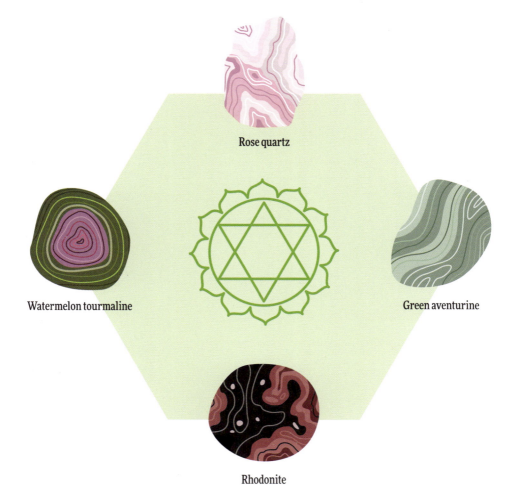

Rose quartz

Watermelon tourmaline

Green aventurine

Rhodonite

Heart Chakra Crystals

Crystals aligned with this energy center are usually green or pink in color and amplify feelings of love, compassion, and emotional healing. These crystals facilitate the flow of unconditional love and empathy, promoting both harmony in relationships and inner peace.

Rose Quartz is renowned for its gentle, nurturing energy that promotes love, compassion, and emotional healing, making it an ideal crystal for fostering harmonious relationships and self-love.

Green Aventurine is valued for its calming and balancing properties, believed to attract luck, prosperity, and opportunities for growth, while also soothing emotional wounds and promoting a sense of wellbeing.

Rhodonite is cherished for its ability to enhance compassion, forgiveness, and emotional balance, supporting the healing of past emotional traumas and promoting self-love and inner harmony.

Watermelon Tourmaline combines the properties of both pink and green tourmaline, fostering a harmonious balance of love and compassion with vitality and creativity. It is believed to cleanse and balance the heart chakra, promoting a sense of inner peace and emotional stability.

Ideas for Use

* Hold the heart chakra crystal in your hand and envision its soothing energy flowing into your chest, where the heart chakra is centered.

* Place this crystal over a body part that you don't give enough love to. Let its loving energy infuse this space with the love you deserve.

* Create a healing crystal grid with other heart chakra stones around your living space. This will foster a nurturing environment that promotes compassion and loving-kindness in all interactions. You can find lots of inspiration for crystals grids online.

Rose essential oil

Geranium essential oil

Marjoram essential oil

Lavender essential oil

Heart Chakra Essential Oils

Essential oils for the heart chakra can help to open, balance, and heal this energy center. By incorporating these heart chakra essential oils into your daily routine, you can promote emotional harmony by connecting to the infinite source of love within you.

Rose essential oil is a hug for your heart. Its gentle and sweet aroma nurtures love, compassion, and emotional wellbeing, soothing grief and bringing sweet comfort to your heart center.

Marjoram essential oil is believed to possess purifying properties that can aid in cleansing negative energies. Sweet and herby, it helps to cultivate emotional balance in the heart chakra.

Lavender essential oil is the ultimate soother. Calming and comforting, it eases tension, releases emotions, and wraps you in a blanket of relaxation, bringing peace to your heart.

Geranium essential oil is your go-to for harmony and love. Floral and balancing, it balances emotions, nurtures the heart, and fosters a sense of connection, making you feel perfectly in tune with yourself and others.

Ideas for Use

* Create a heart chakra room spray by mixing rose essential oil with distilled water in a spray bottle. Mist your space to infuse the air with loving, calming energy. Shake your mist before each use, store in the fridge, and use within one month.

* Put a few drops of a heart chakra essential oil on a cotton ball and place it inside your pillowcase. Let the nurturing scent help you drift into a peaceful and serene sleep.

* Before meditation, gently inhale heart-opening essential oils directly from the bottle.

Chapter 5

The Throat Chakra for Communication and Self-Expression

The Throat Chakra

Located at the throat, the throat chakra is the center of communication, self-expression, and authenticity. It governs our ability to express ourselves verbally and through creative endeavors.

Sanskrit Name: Vishuddha

Meaning: Purification

Element: Ether

Location: Throat

Color: Blue

When Your Throat Chakra is Balanced

* You are able to express your thoughts and emotions clearly and effectively

* You feel comfortable speaking your truth and asserting your opinions

* You express yourself through various forms of art or communication

* You live in alignment with your values and express your true self

* You are able to inspire and motivate others through your words and actions

When Your Throat Chakra is Underactive

* You find it difficult to speak up or express yourself honestly

* You have a fear of judgment or criticism

* You feel unheard and struggle to communicate effectively

* You hold yourself back from sharing ideas or speaking your truth

* You experience creative blockages

When Your Throat Chakra is Overactive

* You talk excessively and may dominate conversations

* You tend to be argumentative

* You speak without considering the impact of your words on others

* You are overly critical of others

* You second-guess your own thoughts and opinions

Physical Symptoms of Throat Chakra Imbalance

* Sore throat or frequent throat infections

* Hoarseness or loss of voice

* Thyroid issues or neck pain

* Jaw tension or teeth grinding

* Issues with the ears

In the analogy of our chakras being likened to our dream home, the throat chakra is akin to communicating to people within the home. Tuning in to our authentic expression and prioritizing clear communication can enhance our interpersonal relationships and create a truly harmonious household, leading to us feeling seen, heard, and understood.

You will need

Pen and paper

A fireproof container
(such as a terracotta pot)

A lighter or matches

Release the Past Ritual

When our throat chakra is out of balance, we may find it hard to communicate freely. Often, this inability to express ourselves has been ignited by forces outside of ourselves. To bring our throat chakra back into balance, we must acknowledge and release ourselves from all the moments that have made us want to keep small and quiet. In this ritual, you will begin to unshackle yourself from any wounding that has diminished the power of your voice in the past.

The Ritual

1 Find a space where you feel relaxed and will be undisturbed.

2 Close your eyes and connect to your breath. Allow your breath to settle into a pattern that feels deep and expansive.

3 Bring your hands to your neck and gently cup your throat. Say aloud 3 times "I honor my voice. It is safe now for me to release all that is blocking my throat. My voice matters."

4 Bring to mind whoever it is who has been a source of wounding for your voice. Maybe it's a friend who told you that you were too loud, or a family member who told you to keep quiet.

5 Take your pen and paper and begin to write a letter to this person. You may want to write about the moment they hurt you, and the impact they've had on your life. Give yourself full permission to feel your feelings. Write down all the things you wish you could say to them.

6 Once you have finished writing your letter, read it out loud.

7 Place your letter in your fireproof container and set the paper alight.

8 Witness the flames engulfing your letter and affirm "I release this story, this person, this wounding from my system. My voice matters. My voice is free."

You will need

Blue candle (representing
the throat chakra)

A mirror

A glass of water or self-expression elixir
(see page 90)

Journal and a pen

Integrity Check Ritual

**We can often tell little white lies or say things we feel
others want to hear in order to keep the peace, but what
about the peace inside of us? Committing to being honest
when you speak can only ever strengthen true connections.
This ritual will aid you in checking whether you are
conducting yourself with integrity and illuminate where
you can begin to honor your truth more.**

The Ritual

1 Take a moment to ground yourself by sitting comfortably.

2 As you light the blue candle, set an intention for your ritual, like: "I am committed to speaking with honesty and integrity."

3 Gaze at the flame and take a few cleansing breaths.

4 Switch your gaze to your mirror and look into your own eyes. Be with yourself for a little while.

5 When you feel ready, speak out loud: "I am truthful with myself and others."

6 Observe and meet with love any feelings or thoughts that make themselves present.

7 Take a drink of your water or healing elixir and imagine it cleansing and energizing your throat.

8 Ask yourself: Where in my life am I not being completely honest?

9 Sit down with your journal. Reflect on the mirror exercise and write freely about any areas in your life where you feel you may not be living with full integrity.

10 Reflect on any steps you can take to bring more honesty and integrity into your life. Write down any commitments or actions you plan to take.

11 Express gratitude for the insights gained during the ritual. Extinguish the candle, thanking it for its light and guidance.

12 Take a few moments to sit quietly, feeling the energy of your throat chakra balanced and clear.

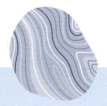

You will need

A water-safe throat chakra crystal
(like blue lace agate or aquamarine)

A glass jar or bottle

Fresh water

Sticky note and a pen (optional)

Self-Expression Elixir

Infusing water with crystals is a powerful way to create healing elixirs that can bring balance and harmony to your body and spirit. If you need to have a difficult conversation or you simply want to feel more confident in your self–expression, make a batch of this water and sip throughout the day to support your throat center. This self expression elixir can be used to accompany any of the throat chakra rituals within this book or simply whenever you feel like you need a boost.

The Ritual

1 Cleanse your throat chakra crystal by rinsing it under cool running water, affirming that it is being purified to become a healing vessel of energy for your throat chakra.

2 Fill your bottle with fresh water.

3 Gently place the cleansed crystal inside your bottle.

4 Hold the bottle in your hands and affirm your intentions for this elixir. Words like "May this elixir help balance and heal my throat chakra so I show up as the most authentic version of myself" will do the trick. Speak whatever words feel true to you.

5 Leave your water bottle for at least 5 hours so that the water can be infused with the healing vibrations of the crystal.

6 When it's ready to drink, remove the crystal.

7 Drink your elixir with full presence and, as you do, envision the energy of the crystal and water flowing through you, opening your throat chakra and empowering your voice.

Throat Chakra Mudra

Granthita mudra, also known as "knot mudra," is a hand gesture that focuses on releasing energetic "knots" and blockages in the throat chakra. Practicing granthita mudra is said to aid in unlocking self-expression, making it a powerful gesture to practice to bring harmony to the throat center.

How to Practice Granthita Mudra

1 Sit comfortably, ensuring your spine is straight and your shoulders are relaxed.

2 Bring your hands into a prayer pose (anjali mudra) at your heart space.

3 Interlace your fingers together and clasp your hands together.

4 In this position, now join your index finger to touch your thumb on each hand. Hold this position.

5 Gently close your eyes or lower your gaze and bring your attention inward to your throat.

6 Connect to your breath, taking slow, deep inhales and exhales.

7 Stay in this position for a few minutes or as long as it feels comfortable.

8 Gently release the mudra by placing your hands palms down on your thighs or knees.

9 Take a moment to feel refreshed and centered in your ability to communicate effectively.

Throat Chakra Mantra

The mantra for the element of ether, which corresponds to the throat chakra, is "HAM." Chanting HAM (pronounced "hum") is believed to cleanse and activate the throat chakra, facilitating clear communication and self-expression. When prana flows freely through the throat chakra, it enables authentic expression of thoughts, feelings, and ideas.

How to Chant HAM

1   Sit in a comfortable position. If possible, keep your spine erect to allow your life force energy to flow freely.

2   Close your eyes and begin to draw your attention inward. Bring your awareness to the center of your throat, where the throat chakra is located.

3   Visualize a blue spinning wheel of energy at this point.

4   Start chanting the mantra HAM aloud.

5   Chant it at a comfortable pitch and volume. Let the sound resonate deeply within you.

6   As you chant, feel the vibration of the sound HAM resonating in the center of your throat. Imagine this vibration clearing and energizing your throat chakra, bringing it into balance.

7   Continue chanting the mantra for 5–10 minutes.

8   After chanting, take a moment to sit quietly and observe any sensations, thoughts, or emotions that arise.

Throat Chakra Affirmations

Affirmations for the throat chakra can aid in clear communication and authentic self-expression. Notice your reactions to these affirmations. Do they inspire you to speak your truth more confidently? How can you create more opportunities for genuine self-expression in your life?

My voice matters.

I speak my truth with confidence and clarity.

I communicate my thoughts and feelings with ease.

I express myself authentically.

I listen to others with compassion and understanding.

My words are aligned with my highest truth.

I am open and honest in my communication.

I trust in my ability to speak my mind.

I share my ideas and knowledge freely.

My voice is strong and powerful.

I speak with kindness and compassion toward myself and others.

I am a good listener.

I am honest in all my communications.

I embrace silence and the power it holds.

I am comfortable speaking in front of others.

Throat Chakra
Journal Prompts

These journaling prompts are an invitation for you to explore and enhance your ability to communicate and express yourself authentically. By engaging with these prompts, you can uncover any areas where you may feel silenced or misunderstood, and work on your ability to listen as well as to communicate.

* Imagine you have stepped into living as the boldest, most fully expressed, unapologetic version of you. Who are you as this person?

* What does your life look like as this person?

* Why are you not living as this version of you now?

* List all of the thoughts you have about yourself that inhibit your self-expression. How can you overcome these blocks?

* Reflect on a situation where you used your voice boldly. How did it feel?

* Reflect on a situation where you suppressed your voice and found it difficult to express your needs. How did it feel?

* If you found yourself in a similar sticky situation, what would you do differently to advocate for yourself?

* Are there any difficult conversations you aren't having? What scares you most about having this conversation?

* What one action could you take today to honor and strengthen your voice?

* What does authentic communication mean to you?

* Who in your life is a role model for honest, truthful, and clear communication? What traits of theirs would you like to embody for yourself?

* Who makes you feel heard?

* Write about a dream or aspiration that you've hesitated to vocalize. What steps can you take to share this dream confidently with others?

Lapis lazuli

Amazonite

Blue lace agate

Aquamarine

Throat Chakra Crystals

Crystals aligned with the throat chakra enhance communication, self-expression, and honesty. Utilizing throat chakra crystals can help alleviate fear of speaking your truth, enhance creativity in verbal and written expression, and encourage harmonious interactions based on mutual understanding and respect.

Lapis Lazuli is prized for its healing properties that promote inner peace, self-expression, and spiritual enlightenment, enhancing clarity of thought and creativity.

Blue Lace Agate is celebrated for its calming and soothing energies that aid in communication, fostering honesty, and enhancing self-confidence.

Aquamarine is valued for its purification and cleansing properties, believed to promote clear communication, harmony in relationships, and inner tranquility.

Amazonite is cherished for its balancing and calming effects, supporting emotional healing, enhancing intuition, and encouraging self-discovery and personal growth.

Ideas for Use

* Hold the throat chakra crystal in your hand and visualize its calming energy flowing into your throat and neck area.

* Hold on to a crystal while journaling to facilitate a free flow of words. If you encounter any blocks, rub the crystal and ask it to help you express yourself without hesitation.

* Place a throat chakra crystal under your pillow or on your bedside table while you sleep. This can facilitate healing and support clear communication in your dreams and subconscious.

Peppermint essential oil

Sage essential oil

Chamomile essential oil

Eucalyptus essential oil

Throat Chakra Essential Oils

Using essential oils can help to open, balance, and heal this vital energy center, enhancing communication, self-expression, and truth. By incorporating specific essential oils into your daily routine, whether by using them (diluted) topically or by diffusing, you can promote clear communication and deepen your connection to your inner voice.

Peppermint essential oil helps clear your mind. Refreshing, invigorating, and stimulating, it encourages mindful and effective communication.

Chamomile essential oil is a real nurturer. Soothing and calming, it can support you in moments when you aren't really feeling like yourself.

Eucalyptus essential oil opens up the pathways of communication. Clear and clarifying, it refreshes the mind and revitalizes the spirit, encouraging honest and authentic expression.

Sage essential oil purifies and strengthens the throat chakra. Wise and empowering, it enhances clarity of speech and promotes integrity in communication, empowering you to speak with wisdom and authority.

Ideas for Use

* Dilute a few drops of your chosen essential oil in a carrier oil (like jojoba or coconut oil) and apply with care and attention to the throat area. Massage in a clockwise direction.

* Add a few drops of your essential oil to a bowl of steaming hot water. Cover your head with a towel and inhale deeply, allowing the steam to penetrate and cleanse the throat chakra.

* Create a throat chakra spray by adding a few drops of your chosen essential oil to a small spray bottle filled with water. Shake well and lightly mist the air around your throat to promote clarity of communication and soothe the throat area.

Chapter 6

The Third Eye Chakra for Intuition and Insight

The Third Eye Chakra

Positioned between the eyebrows, the third eye chakra is the center of intuition, inner wisdom, and spiritual insight. It allows us to enhance our intuition, imagination, and ability to envision possibilities beyond the ordinary.

Sanskrit Name: Ajna

Meaning: Perceive, beyond wisdom

Element: Light

Location: Between the eyebrows

Color: Indigo

When Your Third Eye Chakra is Balanced

* You trust your inner guidance and insights

* You foster creativity and visualize possibilities

* You are intuitive

* You have clarity of mind

* You sense energy and connections beyond the physical realm

When Your Third Eye Chakra is Underactive

* You feel out of touch with your intuition and inner wisdom

* You resist new ideas and perspectives

* You have difficulty concentrating and lack mental clarity

* You feel lost or unsure about your life's direction

When Your Third Eye Chakra is Overactive

* You lose touch with reality and become overly idealistic

* You fixate on spiritual matters or psychic phenomena

* You drain your energy through excessive spiritual practices

Physical Symptoms of Third Eye Chakra Imbalance

* Headaches or migraines

* Vision problems or eye strain

* Sleep disturbances or insomnia

* Dizziness or vertigo

* Sinus issues or allergies

Unlocking the energy of your third eye chakra can be like stepping into an undiscovered area of your dream home, like the attic. Just as exploring the attic can uncover valuable and enlightening discoveries about the house, tapping into the third eye chakra can reveal profound insights and intuitive understanding about yourself and the world around you.

You will need

A candle

A lighter or matches

Mind-Clearing Flame Ritual

Candle gazing, also known as Trataka, is a powerful yogic practice that stimulates the third eye chakra. By focusing your gaze at the steady flame of a candle, engaging in the practice is said to clear mental clutter, improve concentration, and awaken heightened states of awareness.

The Ritual

1 Find a quiet room where you won't be disturbed.

2 Dim the lights to create a calm, serene atmosphere.

3 Place your candle at an arm's length away from you on a stable surface.

4 Light the candle and ensure its flame is burning steady without flickering.

5 Sit in a comfortable position with your spine straight. You can sit cross-legged on the floor or on a chair with your feet flat on the ground. Rest your hands on your knees or in your lap.

6 Focus your gaze on the flame of the candle. Keep your eyes steady and try not to blink.

7 Concentrate on the tip of the wick where the flame is most stable.

8 As you gaze at the flame, allow your mind to become still. Let go of any thoughts or distractions. If your eyes start to water or feel strained, gently close them.

9 With your eyes closed, picture the flame glowing brightly at your third eye chakra. Feel the warmth and light of the flame illuminating this area, clearing away any blockages or stagnant energy.

10 Take slow, deep breaths as you visualize the flame. Or open your eyes and return to gazing at the real flame if you feel able. Inhale deeply through your nose, filling your lungs, and exhale slowly through your mouth.

11 Allow each breath to deepen your relaxation and connection to the third eye chakra.

12 When you feel ready, gently open your eyes and extinguish the candle.

You will need

A small amethyst crystal

Journal and a pen

Soft meditation music (optional)

Intuition Boosting Meditation

In our fast-paced, often chaotic world, it's easy to become disconnected from the wisdom of our own inner guidance. However, your intuition is a powerful tool that is always available to you. By regularly making time and space to practice this ritual, you can tap into your innate ability to see the bigger picture, trust your instincts, and make decisions aligned with your highest good.

The Ritual

1 Find a comfortable place where you can lay down undisturbed.

2 Take your amethyst crystal and gently rub it in circular motions at the third eye point between your eyebrows.

3 Tune in to the intention for this session: to connect deeply with your intuition and open yourself up to your inner wisdom.

4 Leave your crystal gently balanced at your third eye energy center and settle your arms by your side.

5 Connect to your breath and imagine breathing in and exhaling through the crystal on your forehead. Begin to intuitively ask questions in your mind. These can be related to a specific situation you want clarity on or can be more open and generic, such as: What guidance do I need to hear right now? What do I need to know?

6 Listen.

7 Imagine an indigo light emanating from the crystal, swirling around your third eye point, expanding your intuitive awareness.

8 Spend 10–15 minutes in this state, asking questions and listening. Allow thoughts or insights to come through naturally. Trust that your intuition is being awakened.

9 Open your eyes, remove the crystal from your forehead, take your journal and pen and write down any information you received.

10 Over the coming days, pay attention to any intuitive nudges or insights that arise. Trust that your intuition is becoming more attuned and that you are aligning more deeply with your inner wisdom. Repeat this ritual as often as you feel drawn to.

You will need

A dedicated dream journal
or notebook and a pen

A piece of amethyst or another
third eye chakra crystal

1 drop lavender essential oil

Dream Journal Ritual

Connecting with your dreams can be a powerful way to activate and enhance your third eye chakra. By keeping a dream journal, you can tap into the subconscious mind, which is a gateway to the higher realms of consciousness. This ritual not only helps you tap into the wisdom of your dreams but also fosters a greater sense of insight and clarity in your waking life.

The Ritual

1 Before going to sleep, place your dream journal and pen beside your bed.

2 Put a drop of lavender essential oil on a piece of tissue under your pillow with your piece of amethyst.

3 Lay down and get nice and cosy. Let the calming scent of lavender gently lull you to sleep.

4 Upon waking, try to remain still for a few moments, keeping your eyes closed. Recall as much detail as you can from your dreams.

5 Gently reach for your dream journal and begin writing down everything you remember. Don't worry about structure or coherence; just let the memories flow onto the page. If you can't recall your dream, record this too, and write down how you are feeling upon waking.

6 After writing, take a few moments to reflect on your dreams. Look for patterns, symbols, or emotions that stand out. Consider how these might relate to your waking life and your spiritual journey.

7 Write a brief interpretation or any insights you have.

8 Thank your subconscious mind and the universe for the insights gained from your dreams. Affirm your commitment to continuing this practice and strengthening your third eye chakra.

9 At the end of each week, review your entries to look for recurring themes or messages or anything that relates to the way your week has unfolded. This ongoing practice will deepen your connection to your intuition and the third eye chakra.

Third Eye Chakra Mudra

Kalesvara mudra, also known as "monkey mind mudra," is a gesture used to activate and balance the energy of the third eye chakra. Practicing kalesvara mudra is said to calm down the "monkey mind" and clear conflicting thoughts so that we can have deeper clarity in our minds.

How to Practice Kalesvara Mudra

1 Sit comfortably, ensuring your spine is straight and your shoulders are relaxed.

2 Bring your hands into a prayer pose (anjali mudra) at your heart space.

3 Part your palms slightly.

4 Join the tips of your thumbs together and, keeping them extended, point them downward.

5 Now, curl all of your fingers so that it resembles a heart, with the first joints of your fingers and nails touching.

6 Extend your middle fingers and join their fingertips together gently.

7 Hold this position.

8 Gently close your eyes or lower your gaze and bring your attention inward.

9 Connect to your breath, taking slow, deep inhales and exhales.

10 Stay in this position for a few minutes or as long as it feels comfortable.

11 Gently release the mudra by placing your hands palms down on your thighs or knees.

12 Take a moment to feel the effects of clearing your mind to attune to your inner compass.

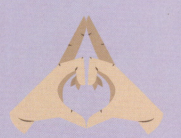

Third Eye Chakra Mantra

The third eye chakra is beyond all elements so the mantra for this energy center is "OM"—the primordial sound of the universe. Chanting OM (pronounced "A-U-M") is believed to cleanse and activate the third eye chakra, enhancing intuition, inner wisdom, and spiritual insight. When prana flows freely through the third eye chakra, it fosters clarity of vision and deeper perception beyond the physical realm.

How to Chant OM

1 Sit in a comfortable position. If possible, keep your spine erect to allow your life force energy to flow freely.

2 Close your eyes and begin to draw your attention inward.

3 Bring your awareness to the point between your eyebrows where the third eye chakra is located.

4 Visualize a purple spinning wheel of energy at this point.

5 Start chanting the mantra OM aloud. Chant it at a comfortable pitch and volume. Let the sound resonate deeply within you.

6 As you chant, feel the vibration of the sound OM resonating in the center of your eyebrows. Imagine this vibration clearing and energizing your third eye chakra, bringing it into balance.

7 Continue chanting the mantra for 5–10 minutes.

8 After chanting, take a moment to sit quietly and observe any sensations, thoughts, or emotions that arise.

Third Eye Chakra Affirmations

Affirmations for the third eye chakra can elevate your trust in listening to your own inner compass and intuition. How do you feel in your head and your heart as you affirm these words? Is there a disconnect between the two? Do you believe these words to be true?

I trust my intuition.

I trust my inner wisdom and follow it confidently.

My mind is clear and focused.

I see the truth in all situations.

I am open to signs from the universe.

I trust the messages I receive from my higher self.

My intuition guides me to the right decisions.

I trust myself.

My intuition is a powerful tool.

I am open to new ideas and insights.

I am connected to universal wisdom.

My intuition is strong and reliable.

I can manifest my visions for my life.

I am aware of my higher purpose.

I trust the divine timing of my life's journey.

Third Eye Chakra
Journal Prompts

These journaling prompts invite you to explore and deepen your connection to your intuition, inner wisdom, and imagination. By engaging with these prompts, you can uncover any areas where you may feel disconnected from your intuition or lack clarity, and begin to cultivate a more intuitive and visionary perspective.

* What does intuition mean to you?

* Do you feel like you have a strong intuition? Why or why not?

* Reflect on a time you followed your intuition and it led you to something wonderful. What did your intuition feel like in that moment?

* Reflect on a moment that you ignored your intuition and wished you hadn't. What did you learn from that experience?

* What are five things you intuitively know about yourself?

* What situations in your life do you wish you had more clarity on?

* In what ways could you receive more clarity on these situations?

* Write about a vivid dream you've had that you still remember. Do you feel this dream had any insights or wisdom to offer? Does it still?

* Do you notice any recurring signs, patterns, or synchronicities in your daily life? What do you feel they mean?

* What ways can you cultivate mindfulness and presence in your daily life?

* Do you trust where you are on your journey right now? Why or why not?

* Is there anything you feel that is blocking you from accessing your inner truths?

* Tuning in to your inner wisdom, what do you know to be true, if anything, about your future?

* What would you like your future to entail?

Sodalite

Lepidolite

Amethyst

Kyanite

Third Eye Chakra Crystals

Crystals linked to the third eye chakra can deepen meditation practice and foster a clearer connection to inner wisdom and higher consciousness. Using these crystals within rituals or in your day-to-day routines can help open pathways to expanded consciousness and heightened spiritual awareness.

Sodalite possesses healing properties that enhance intuition, mental clarity, and self-expression, promoting harmony in communication and fostering inner peace.

Amethyst is renowned for its calming and protective qualities that facilitate spiritual growth, intuition, and emotional stability, supporting clarity of mind and relaxation.

Kyanite promotes balance, tranquility, and inner alignment, aiding in communication and fostering a deep sense of self-awareness.

Lepidolite offers calming energies that support emotional healing, stress relief, and inner peace, enhancing awareness and promoting a sense of balance and stability.

Ideas for Use

* Hold the third eye chakra crystal in your hand and visualize its illuminating energy flowing into your forehead, where the third eye chakra resides.

* Meditate with the crystal positioned over this area to enhance intuition and inner wisdom.

* Create a sacred space with other third eye chakra stones around your meditation area to deepen your spiritual practices and strengthen your connection to higher consciousness, facilitating clearer insights in your daily life.

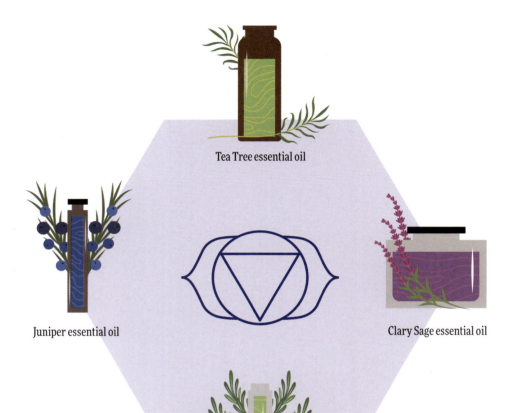

Tea Tree essential oil

Juniper essential oil

Clary Sage essential oil

Rosemary essential oil

Third Eye Essential Oils

Using essential oils can help to open, balance, and heal the third eye chakra , enhancing intuition, insight, and inner wisdom. By incorporating specific essential oils into your daily routine, you can promote spiritual awareness and deepen your connection to your higher self.

Tea Tree essential oil has a pungent and medicinal scent that is known for its grounding properties. It can help to deepen meditation and enhance intuition.

Clary Sage is sweet and herbaceous and is an essential oil is known for its ability to enhance vision and clarity, making it an excellent choice for supporting the third eye chakra.

Rosemary essential oil has a strong medicinal scent that can aid mental clarity and focus, helping to clear the mind for deeper intuitive insights.

Juniper essential oil is earthy and sweet and known for its ability to cleanse and protect, making it useful for clearing any energetic blockages in the third eye chakra.

Ideas for Use

* Combine essential oils with visualization techniques during meditation. Envision a bright indigo light filling your third eye area as you inhale the scent of the oils, helping to deepen your intuition and inner wisdom.

* Dilute essential oils by mixing them with carrier oil (like jojoba or coconut oil) and apply them to the forehead between the eyebrows, where the third eye chakra is located.

* Before meditation, place a drop of diluted essential oil in your palms, rub them together, and then cup your hands over your nose and mouth. Inhale deeply to awaken and align the third eye chakra.

Chapter 7

The Crown Chakra for Spirituality and Connection

The Crown Chakra

Located at the top of the head, the crown chakra is our connection to the divine, spiritual wisdom, and higher consciousness. It transcends the ego and represents our spiritual enlightenment and unity with the universe.

Sanskrit Name: Sahasrara

Meaning: Thousand-petaled

Element: Ether

Location: Top of your head

Color: Violet or white

When Your Crown Chakra is Balanced

* You have a sense of oneness with the universe and all beings

* You embrace spirituality and experience inner peace

* You welcome new ideas and higher wisdom

* You live in harmony with your higher purpose and spiritual path

When Your Crown Chakra is Underactive

* You feel spiritually adrift or cut off from higher guidance

* You doubt spiritual truths or dismiss higher wisdom

* You resist spiritual growth

* You feel lost or lacking purpose in life

When Your Crown Chakra is Overactive

* You feel disconnected from reality

* You cling rigidly to spiritual beliefs or ideologies

* You feel spiritually superior or detached from worldly concerns

* You overthink spiritual matters and feel overwhelmed by cosmic energies

* You struggle to integrate spiritual experiences into daily life

Physical Symptoms of Crown Chakra Imbalance

* Headaches or migraines

* Sensitivity to light and sound

* Neurological disorders

* Issues with the pineal gland or hypothalamus

* Insomnia

Caring for the crown chakra is like gazing through the skylight of your dream home and up at the stars. Just as stargazing opens your mind to the vastness of the universe, a balanced crown chakra expands your consciousness beyond earthly limitations.

You will need

Magazines, catalogues, or printed images

Scissors

A large piece of paper

Glue

Pens

Your Highest Self Moodboard

Who did you come here to be? What is the most divine expression of all that you are? This ritual is all about tuning in to your highest self and creating a moodboard that captures your most authentic, elevated essence. The crown chakra is the gateway to this divine connection, linking you to the infinite wisdom of the universe and your true purpose. Think of it as a fun and creative way to align with your inner wisdom and dreams.

The Ritual

1 Choose a quiet and comfortable space and spread your creative materials out within easy reach.

2 Place your hands on the top of your head, where your crown chakra is.

3 Close your eyes and visualize a beam of white or violet light descending from the universe into your crown chakra. Say: "I am open to connecting with my highest self and aligning with my dreams and aspirations."

4 Feel this divine energy filling you with clarity, wisdom, and spiritual connection. Allow yourself to receive guidance and inspiration from your highest self. Be open to the wisdom you receive. Let yourself be surprised by what comes through.

5 Gather your magazines, newspapers, and printed images and find photos that reflect your ideal self and life.

6 Cut out images and words that deeply resonate with you, and evoke positive feelings and a sense of alignment with your highest self.

7 Take your large piece of paper and arrange and stick all your images in a way that feels good to you.

8 Sit back and take a moment to observe your moodboard once it's complete. How does it make you feel? What emotions feel present? Does this creation feel true to you? Each day, you can look at your moodboard and imagine all of the images coming to life. Think of steps you can take to become this person.

9 Repeat this ritual whenever you want to update or add to your moodboard, to continue aligning with new versions of your highest self.

You will need

Comfortable clothing for the outdoors

A blanket or mat

A pillow

Cosmic Connection Ritual

If you are feeling lost, lift your gaze to the skies. Sky gazing is a timeless practice that allows you to connect with the infinite universe, transcending the boundaries of your everyday life. As you stare into the heavens above, you can begin to sense the profound connection between your inner self and the boundless universe, a reminder that we are all a piece of something far greater than ourselves. Embrace a sense of wonder in knowing you are inextricably intertwined with the beauty of the universe.

The Ritual

1 Choose a natural setting where you feel at peace. This could be a forest, a beach, a park, or your own yard.

2 Once you arrive at your spot, lay out your blanket and pillow, and lay down and get comfortable .

3 With your eyes closed, begin to connect to your breath and your intentions for your sky gazing session. This could be seeking spiritual guidance, connecting with the universe or simply appreciating the beauty of the world around you.

4 With each inhale, imagine drawing in the divine energy of the universe through the top of your head. With each exhale, release any barriers between you and this energy.

5 Open your eyes and focus on the sky. Allow your gaze to soften and take in the entire expanse above you. Notice the clouds, the birds, and the sky.

6 As you gaze, engage all your senses. Feel the temperature of the air on your skin, listen to the sound of nature around you, notice any scents carried by the breeze. Engaging all your senses will help anchor your connection to the present moment.

7 Visualize a radiant light streaming down from the sky and through the top of your head. Visualize this light streaming down, to touch all living things.

8 Gaze for as long as feels comfortable. Express a moment of gratitude for the experience and carry this sense of divine connection with you as you return to your daily life.

You will need

2 tbsp jojoba oil

Mini glass roll-on bottle

3 drops lavender essential oil

2 drops frankincense essential oil

2 drops myrrh essential oil

Reconnecting Oil Blend

If you are feeling disconnected from yourself, others, or the universe, this crown chakra oil blend is the perfect remedy to support you into a state of reconnection. You can use this essential oil blend as an accompaniment for any of the crown chakra rituals or if you ever need support on your spiritual path.

The Ritual

1 Find a clean, quiet space where you can focus without distractions.

2 Gather all your ingredients and tools.

3 Pour the jojoba oil directly into your roll-on bottle.

4 Add your drops of essential oils.

5 Add the lid and gently mix the oil blend by tilting it up and down.

6 Your oil blend can be applied directly to the top of your scalp or by the base of your neck for use in any of the crown chakra rituals, or in any moment you may feel disconnected from yourself, others, or the universe.

7 As you apply your oil, you may wish to ponder the following questions: What does connection mean to me? In what areas of my life do I feel disconnected? How can I cultivate a deeper connection with myself, others, and the universe?

8 Take a moment to remind yourself that, even though at times it may not feel like it, you are supported by the universe and connected to a greater whole. Carry this feeling of connection with you as you apply your blend. Take this with you throughout your day, knowing that guidance and love are always available to you.

Crown Chakra Mudra

Dhyana mudra, also known as "meditation mudra," is a gesture that is particularly beneficial to the crown chakra since it aids meditation and contemplation, and enhances spiritual connection. The bowl shape you create with your hands in this mudra is said to symbolize that you are ready to receive your blessings. When you practice this mudra, set an intention and signal to the universe that you are ready to receive them.

How to Practice Dhyana Mudra

1   Sit comfortably, ensuring your spine is straight and your shoulders are relaxed.

2   Bring your left hand to rest over your pubis, keeping the palm facing up toward the sky. Gently bring over your right hand and nestle it inside the left.

3   Allow both thumbs to touch each other, pointing upward, so that a triangular shape is formed.

4   Hold this position.

5   Gently close your eyes or lower your gaze and bring your attention inward.

6   Connect to your breath, taking slow, deep inhales and exhales.

7   Stay in this position for a few minutes or as long as it feels comfortable.

8   Gently release the mudra by placing your hands palms-down on your thighs or knees.

9   Slowly open your eyes and bring your awareness back to the present moment, feeling centered and connected to the universe and higher states of consciousness.

Crown Chakra Mantra

Just like the third eye chakra, the crown chakra is beyond all elements so the mantra for this energy center is also "OM"—the primordial sound of the universe. Chanting OM (pronounced "A-U-M") is believed to purify and elevate the crown chakra, facilitating the free flow of divine energy and enhancing spiritual connection and awareness. When prana flows unobstructed through the crown chakra, it fosters a profound sense of unity with the universe and spiritual enlightenment.

How to Chant OM

1 Sit in a comfortable position. If possible, keep your spine erect to allow your life force energy to flow freely.

2 Close your eyes and begin to draw your attention inward. Bring your awareness to the point above your head where the crown chakra is located.

3 Visualize a bright white spinning wheel of energy at this point.

4 Start chanting the mantra OM aloud. Chant it at a comfortable pitch and volume. Let the sound resonate deeply within you.

5 As you chant, feel the vibration of the sound OM resonating above the top of your head. Imagine this vibration clearing and energizing your crown chakra, bringing it into balance.

6 Continue chanting the mantra for 5–10 minutes.

7 After chanting, take a moment to sit quietly and observe any sensations, thoughts, or emotions that arise.

Crown Chakra Affirmations

Crown chakra affirmations can help you connect
with higher wisdom and spiritual awareness. Reflect
on your feelings as you speak these words. Do they
evoke a sense of spiritual alignment and unity with
the universe? How does that make you feel?

I am connected to the divine source
of the universe.

❁

I am one with all that is.

❁

My spirit is free and limitless.

❁

I am in tune with my higher self.

❁

I trust the process of life.

❁

I honor the sacredness of myself
and all other beings.

❁

I am guided by divine wisdom.

❁

I am at peace with myself and
the universe.

❁

I am open to divine guidance.

❁

I am a spiritual being having a
human experience.

❁

I am an important part of this world.

❁

My life is guided by a higher power.

❁

I am open to the abundance of
the universe.

❁

I am aligned with my
highest purpose.

❁

I am grateful for the divine energy
that flows through me.

❁

Crown Chakra
Journal Prompts

These journaling prompts are an invitation for you to explore and deepen your connection to your higher self, spirituality, and universal consciousness. By engaging with these prompts, you can uncover any areas where you may feel spiritually disconnected or lacking in purpose, and begin to cultivate a more profound and expansive sense of spiritual connection.

* What does spirituality mean to you?

* Do you believe in a connection to a higher power?

* If so, how do you cultivate and nurture your connection to the divine or higher power?

* Reflect on a moment when you felt a sense of deep connection to the universe. What allowed you to feel that connection?

* In what ways could you open yourself up to feel that connection to the universe more often?

* In what ways do you integrate spirituality into your daily life?

* Do you feel you are an important part of the universe? Explain why you feel that way.

* What do you feel, if anything, is your life's purpose?

* Do you feel connected to your life's purpose? Why or why not?

* Recall a difficult moment in your life. Did your spiritual beliefs provide solace during this time?

* How do you embody spiritual principles like compassion, gratitude, and forgiveness in your interactions and relationships?

* What does it mean to you to live a life that is spiritually fulfilling?

* What are your own aspirations for spiritual growth?

* What do you need to let go of in order to forge a deeper spiritual connection?

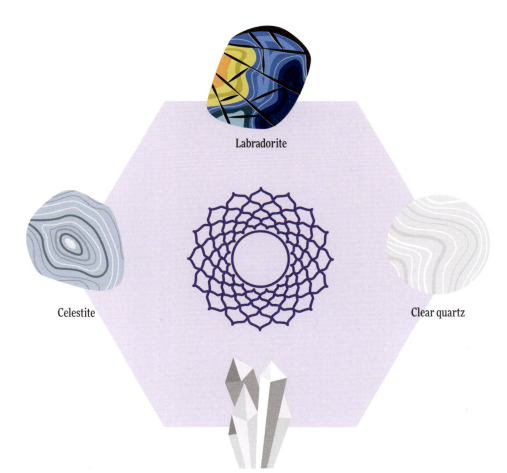

Labradorite

Celestite

Clear quartz

Apophyllite

Crown Chakra Crystals

Crystals for the crown chakra serve as powerful tools to enhance your spiritual connection and elevate your consciousness. These stones are known for their ability to open the mind to higher states of awareness, facilitating a deeper connection to the universe and your higher self.

Labradorite is a popular crystal due to its beautiful iridescent colors. It is known for its mystical healing properties, which enhance intuition, psychic abilities, and spiritual awakening, fostering a deeper connection to inner wisdom and higher realms.

Clear Quartz stands out for its versatile master healing qualities, which amplify energy, clarity of mind, and spiritual awareness, making it an essential crystal for cleansing, purifying, and balancing the chakras.

Apophyllite radiates calming and uplifting properties, which facilitate spiritual growth, inner peace, and emotional healing, promoting a serene and balanced energy field.

Celestite brings a soothing and harmonizing energy, which encourages communication with divine guidance and inner tranquillity, supporting mental clarity and spiritual alignment.

Ideas for Use

* Hold the crown chakra crystal in your hand and envision its radiant energy streaming into the top of your head.

* Write a letter to the universe expressing your desires for spiritual growth or insight. Hold your crown chakra crystal while doing this, to enhance your intention.

* Sleep with your crown chakra crystal under your pillow, to strengthen your connection to divinity while you sleep.

Frankincense essential oil

Holy Basil essential oil

Myrrh essential oil

Neroli essential oil

Crown Chakra Essential Oils

The enchanting aromas of these essential oils can help create sacred spaces for you to carry out your spiritual practices. By incorporating these rich and potent crown chakra essential oils into your life, you can deepen your connection to the divine.

Frankincense is a spicy and fragrant essential oil known for its profound spiritual properties. It helps to elevate the mind and deepen meditation, promoting a sense of divine connection.

Myrrh essential oil is known for its grounding and spiritual qualities. Its sweet and woody qualities aid in the connection to higher realms and promoting a sense of peace.

Neroli essential oil is known for its calming and heart-opening properties. Its refreshing floral aroma supports emotional balance and spiritual connection.

Holy Basil essential oil is an invigorating and fresh scent that supports a balanced state of mind, fostering a deep sense of inner stillness and connection to the divine.

Ideas for Use

* Create a soothing pillow spray by mixing a few drops of lavender or chamomile essential oil with diluted water in a spray bottle. Spritz your pillow before bedtime to promote relaxation and enhance dream states, which can be beneficial for crown chakra alignment during sleep. Shake the spray before use, keep in the fridge, and use within one month.

* Infuse essential oils into an affirmation ritual focused on the crown chakra. Repeat affirmations like "I am connected to divine wisdom" while inhaling the oils.

* Create a massage oil blend. Dilute a few drops of essential oil in a carrier oil (like coconut or jojoba oil) and massage gently into the scalp, neck, and shoulders. This can help release tension and promote clarity of mind.

Conclusion

Balancing your chakras through the rituals offered in this book is not a one-time endeavor, but a lifelong practice of tending to your energetic health. Each tool you've learned is a stepping stone on your path to deeper self-awareness and holistic wellbeing.

There will be times when your chakras are vibrant and spinning freely, and other times when they may feel blocked or out of balance. This is a natural part of life's ebb and flow. Embrace these fluctuations with compassion and patience, knowing that each moment offers a new opportunity for growth and healing.

As you continue on this journey, allow yourself to experiment with new ways to bring balance to your system. Remember, you are your own greatest healer. There is no right or wrong way to care for your chakras, only what feels true and supportive for you in each moment.

It is the greatest honor to be a small part of your healing journey. As you harness the energy of your chakras, may you find strength in grounding, joy in creativity, confidence in your power, love in your heart, truth in your voice, clarity in your vision, and divine connection in your spirit.

With deepest gratitude and all the love in the world,

Lucy x

Recommended Reading

Heart Minded: How to Hold Yourself and Others in Love,
Sarah Blondin, Sounds True, 2020

The Artist's Way: A Spiritual Path to Higher Creativity,
Julia Cameron, Souvenir Press, 2020

**The Seven Spiritual Laws of Success: A Practical Guide to the
Fulfilment of Your Dreams**, Deepak Chopra, Bantam Press, 1996

Untamed: Stop Pleasing, Start Living, Glennon Doyle,
Vermilion, 2020

You Were Never Broken: Poems to Save Your Life, Jeff Foster,
Sounds True, 2020

Loving What Is: Four Questions that can Save Your Life,
Byron Katie, Rider, 2002

Radical Self-Care: Rituals for Inner Resilience, Rebecca Moore,
Leaping Hare Press, 2024

Self-Compassion: The Proven Power of Being Kind to Yourself,
Kristin Neff, Yellow Kite, 2011

The Way of Reiki: The Inner Teachings of Mikao Usui, Frans Stiene,
O Books, 2022

A New Earth: Awakening to Your Life's Purpose, Eckhart Tolle,
Michael Joseph, 2005

Acknowledgments

I would like to express my deepest gratitude to my beautiful mum, dad, and sister (Theresa, Ian, and Sophie Lee) and my best friend in the entire universe (Emilia Romano) who are the best cheerleading team anyone could ever ask for and who supported me endlessly throughout the journey of writing this book.

I am immensely grateful to the team at Leaping Hare Press and Quarto for all their help with this project, with a particular thank-you to my editor Chloe Murphy who has been a complete dream come true to work with.

Finally, to you, lovely reader, thank you for picking up this book. I hope it brings you as much joy and magic as it did for me to write it.

About the Author

Lucy Lee is the founder of The Come As You Are Club, a space where disconnection is replaced by belonging, where authenticity reigns supreme, and where healing can be made joyful. Through the transformative practices of Reiki, sound healing, sharing circles, and social meetups, she crafts environments where every soul is cherished, every heart is embraced, and every being finds solace. No matter the path you're on or the challenges you face, Lucy's spaces are a sanctuary where you will be embraced and held in the fullness of all that you are.

Instagram @comeasyouareclub

About the Illustrator

Viki Lester of Forensics and Flowers is a digital artist from London. Her training in graphic design has led to her bold illustration style, inspired by magic, botanicals, gothic art, and bright colors.

She is is the illustrator of *Practical Crystals* and *Practical Symbols*.

Instagram @forensicsandflowers

Index